C000230922

Planted

Planted

A CHEF'S SHOW-STOPPING VEGAN RECIPES

Chantelle Nicholson

Photography by Nassima Rothacker

Kyle Books

First published in Great Britain in 2018
by Kyle Cathie Limited
Part of Octopus Publishing Group Limited
Carmelite House, 50 Victoria Embankment
London EC4Y 0DZ
www.kylebooks.co.uk

10 9 8 7 6 5 4 3 2 1

ISBN 978 0 85783 448 5

Project Editor: **Kyle Cathie**
Assistant Editor: **Hannah Coughlin**
Copy Editor: **Stephanie Evans**
Designer: **Lucy Gowans**
Photographer: **Nassima Rothacker**
Illustrator: **Lucy Gowans**
Prop Stylist: **Wei Tang**
Food Stylists: **Chantelle Nicholson** and **Becks Wilkinson**
Production: **Nic Jones** and **Gemma John**

A Cataloguing in Publication record for this title is available
from the British Library.

Colour reproduction by Alta, London
Printed and bound in China by 1010
International Printing Ltd.

Ingredient notes
Herbs – a standard bunch is 25g
Non-dairy milk – unsweetened milk, ideally rice milk
or almond milk
Non-dairy butter – sunflower spread is preferable
Onions – medium sized
Nuts – skin on, unless specified

Contents

SPRING

SUMMER

AUTUMN

WINTER

Introduction

To me, veganism encapsulates a lifestyle choice, which excludes using animals for food, clothing or any other purpose, be it a bee or an Iberico pig. However, plant-based eating is based on a diet rich in all things that come from a plant, and not from any animal source. It does not seek to advocate anything more or less. It is rather simple in its form. But in all of this, we cannot forget we are talking about food. To me, food is so much more than just nutrients I put in my body. It is a great source of enjoyment, of creativity, of fun, of friendship and of delicious tastes and flavours. This trumps all. That is why I wrote this book to celebrate delicious food, and to be able to enjoy it.

If you are starting out on a more plant-based lifestyle then it is important you get the vitamins and minerals required for a healthy diet. There are a lot of comments floating around regarding the lack of protein in a plant-based diet. Whilst at present (yes, watch this space) there is no like for like, weight for weight, alternative to animal protein, you can lead a healthy lifestyle which includes protein on a plant-based diet. I am not a qualified nutritionist, nor purport to be, so I would suggest a quick internet search, where there is a plethora of information at your fingertips. In layman's terms, protein is essential for our body to function, it builds and repairs. Along with fat and carbohydrates, it plays a tripartite role in keeping us alive. It also plays a very interesting role in the science behind cookery, and chemical reactions. Protein can be found in both animal products and plant based products, hence the forceful reasoning that you can get enough protein from a plant based diet to function, and to perform well. Plant-based eating is becoming more common in top performing athletes, which to me solidifies the notion above.

As a child, growing up on the North Island in New Zealand, fruit and vegetables were a big feature of early life. Time spent outside was the norm, with a warm climate that enabled this most of the year. With a backyard and a neighbourhood where all the children spent time together, the outdoors was our playground. Being in the garden, picking the sour, green grapes off the vine, or peeling the insect-like outer leaves off a Cape Gooseberry before the sweet, juicy sphere popped in my mouth remain entrenched in my memory. Picking our vegetables for dinner or nipping out to the garden for some fresh mint to put in with the potatoes were just part and parcel of growing up. The summer holidays spent on my Uncle and Aunty's stone fruit orchard and sheep farm in Central Otago were a long, happy and sunny sabbatical of family time and growing fruit as a livelihood. Looking back on it now, I see it for the education, privilege and wonderful experience that it was, and that in today's society is

not the norm. My earliest childhood memories are mostly all about food. Understanding where food came from was the rule, not the exception, which I think steered me to life as a chef and an advocate of food, nutrition and cookery.

A few years into my Law and Commerce degrees in Dunedin, I decided that the burning fire in my belly, in relation to how much I loved cooking, was not to be dampened. Plus, as a self-funded student, I needed a job. So approached my favourite local café, aptly named Ground Essence, advising I had zero experience but loved to cook. Luckily for me, they happened to be looking for a part-time cook and the two female owners took a chance on me. My muffin-making skills improved and I started to work with the owners to develop a more extended weekend brunch menu, from a kitchen that was approximately 1 x 2m, including the dishwasher and the domestic oven. A little ambitious, but it was a success mostly, and the beginning of the journey.

In 2001, the university summer holidays arrived and I needed more work, so applied for a kitchen hand job at Corstorphine House, a boutique hotel and restaurant with its own kitchen garden (a no brainer in those days). The head chef, Craig, ended up employing me as a chef and thus my education in elements of classic French cuisine began, (he had trained under a French chef and had spent time in the U.K.) from beurre blanc, to a classic beef stock to tarte au citron.

After finishing my university studies I had the cooking bug well and truly, but a little word from my mother encouraged me to 'at least give being a lawyer a go, and get your bar exam under your belt'. Moving to Wellington, I did just that. Part way through my studies, whilst working as an Investigator for the Banking Ombudsman, I spotted an advertisement in our national foodie bible, *Cuisine Magazine*, for Gordon Ramsay's Chefsearch competition. Contemplating it for all of a minute, I set to work creating a 3 course menu with recipes and duly posted it off. A couple of months later I received an unexpected phone call, inviting me to the semi finals of the competition, to be held in a few weeks' time. Excitement soon turned to anxiety, realising I had not been in a restaurant kitchen for over 18 months. Suffice to say, with a little kiwi ambition and confidence, I made it through to the final six contestants. The night of the final, I was chatting to one of the judges, a fellow kiwi called Josh Emett, who was head chef of the Savoy Grill in London. As is typical in NZ, it turned out we had one degree of separation between us. He offered me a job on the spot. Not thinking twice, I jumped on the opportunity and arrived in London in September 2004.

Reflecting on my fourteen years in London is an interesting exercise. I stayed at the Savoy Grill until Josh left in 2006, when Marcus Wareing, knowing my admiration for Josh, took me over to his restaurant in Knightsbridge, Pétrus. Stepping up a level, here I honed my chef skills further but, perhaps more importantly in terms of my future, I showed Marcus that I wasn't just a professionally-trained chef, but a lawyer too. This led to opportunities both inside and outside the kitchen, supporting him in cookery book writing, external events, and the kitchen as a whole, as well as the business transition in 2009 where he became an independent operator.

Fast forward to 2010, an email arrived in Marcus's inbox about a project in King's Cross, which at that time was a not-so-desirable part of London that had embarked upon the journey of gentrification. Marcus, Jane (his wife) and I went to look at a derelict building site, which held all the promise of the glory it once was as the Midland Grand Hotel, designed by Sir George Gilbert Scott. After many discussions – and a decision on my part that I needed a different type of experience in terms of the restaurant world – I opened our new restaurant, The Gilbert Scott, as General Manager, thus out of my whites. Whilst I designed the opening menu, scouring historical British cookbooks, I spent little time in the kitchen and learnt all about Grade 1-listed buildings, reservations, marketing, restaurant operations, financial control, IT and general maintenance, to name but a small part of my education. A swift and in-depth learning curve is the best way to describe it, invaluably so in hindsight.

In 2013 we decided, as a group, that we had some great people around us, and to develop them further another site was needed. After a pre-theatre dinner with a good friend before the English

National Opera at The Coliseum, I chanced upon an empty restaurant site in Seven Dials, Covent Garden, London. Today, this is Tredwells. Still out of whites, I managed the opening process from finding the site to opening the doors in September 2014.

In February 2015, we had to make a change in the running of the kitchen at The Gilbert Scott. We had a great sous chef at Tredwells so offered him the reins. I spent 2 months in the kitchen, showing him the ropes. In April, my then head chef at Tredwells decided, after a rather tough opening, that the role was not for him. Needing to get the restaurant back on track to ensure it stayed in line with our company ethos – great food and drink with hospitable service – and knowing the best place to do that was from the engine room, the kitchen, I stepped back in. I thought it would be a temporary move whilst a new head chef was recruited, but I soon learnt that I could do the two things I enjoyed most, being in a kitchen and managing business operations. I realised the white jacket was part of me, and it was where I felt at my most comfortable and confident. Being able to cook and create, as well as bring people around me to inspire and develop, is for me, where I am happiest.

Throughout my journey with Marcus, I have been involved in many, many things. I co-authored all of his cookery books, leading me to where I am today, in writing my first solo book. Why a plant-based book, you may ask? Needing to face this query, as opposed to just doing what felt right, I have realised it is part of where I am from, and part of where I want to go. Good nutrition is, on the most basic of levels, the difference between life and death. Spending time at the 2017 Global Nutrition Summit, in Milan, opened my eyes even further to this, and how much more needs to be done to ensure global malnutrition is tackled and overcome. A large part of good nutrition is about nutrients, and plants have some of the densest nutrient rich sources such as kale, garlic, seaweed, blueberries and cocoa. Whilst I am not here to debate environmental issues I do feel it is something we need to be conscious of, and act according to that level of conscious thought and understanding.

In terms of the recipes in *Planted*, they are categorised into seasons, as I do believe food tastes much better when it is eaten in the season it was grown in. Ripeness can be underrated, as can seasonality, but both need to be brought to the forefront. 95 per cent of all ingredients in this book are available from the supermarket, but I would encourage you to visit your local farmer's market if you can, to cook with seasonal produce. It will taste better, for sure. If you can get produce that is local to where you are from, this will also have an impact on more than just the nutritional value; it has a positive benefit on environmental and local sustainability too.

All recipes in this book are approachable. Some may have more steps than others, and more ingredients than others, but they are all created to be able to produce a great tasting plate of food. It can be a little frustrating, as a cook, to have to purchase ingredients that are difficult to source, and are only used once so I have made an effort not to do this. You will also notice the prevalence of fresh herbs in a lot of my recipes. Try and grow some of these yourself. Rosemary, thyme and bay are all hardy herbs that generally can do pretty well in all climates. Being able to snip a few sprigs off will save you time, money and any potential wastage. And the flavour of these herbs really will enhance the dishes, so please try not to substitute with dried ones, or leave them out!

One ingredient I must mention, which you may not have heard of in this guise, is aquafaba. Aquafaba is the thick, watery substance that results from cooking legume seeds. I cannot profess to know much about its scientific properties but I know a lot about its culinary functions in that it can be used an almost exact substitute for egg whites. I generally use it from cans of chickpeas; you just need to strain it through a fine sieve and it is ready. I read about it on twitter about 18 months ago, and doubted it would be as good as it is. It was a rather wonderful discovery when I made my first batch of meringues with it.

Do add your own touches to the recipes and don't be afraid to try something new or different. Food is a journey, not a destination, so above all, enjoy making it and enjoy eating it.

Breakfast & Brunch

Seeded Granola and Chai-spiced Poached Plums

Homemade granola is super simple and has a good shelf life when kept in an airtight container. Dark red plums are among my favourite fruits to poach, so I suggest doing a four times recipe and keeping a large container in the fridge – perfect for breakfast and pudding.

Serves 4

For the plums

8 plums

50g caster sugar

2 English Breakfast tea bags

1 cinnamon stick

4 cardamom pods

2 star anise

4 cloves

1 bay leaf

For the granola

150g rolled oats

60g coconut oil

40g sesame seeds

40g sunflower seeds

60g pumpkin seeds

60g dates, chopped

½ teaspoon fennel seeds

½ teaspoon salt

2 tablespoons agave syrup

non-dairy yogurt, to serve

Preheat the oven to 170°C/fan 150°C/gas mark 3.

First prepare the plums. Cut each plum in half, remove the stone and set aside. Put the sugar in a large saucepan or deep frying pan with 250ml warm water. Bring to the boil, then add the tea bags, cinnamon stick, cardamom pods, star anise, cloves and bay leaf. Simmer for 3 minutes, then remove from the heat and allow to steep for 6 minutes. Lift out the tea bags and return the pan to the heat. Bring to a simmer, then add the plums, cut-side down. Cover with a lid and simmer gently for 5–7 minutes, until just soft. Remove from the heat, allow to cool slightly, then peel off the skins and transfer to a container and refrigerate.

For the granola, put all the ingredients except the agave into a deep roasting tray and cook for 8–12 minutes, stirring every couple of minutes, until golden. Drizzle over the agave and toast for a further 4 minutes. Remove from the oven and allow to cool.

Serve the granola with the plums and a spoonful of yogurt.

Potato, Celeriac, Onion Seed and Thyme Rostis with HP Gravy

Traditionally, rostis are made with potato, but I really like the addition of the earthy celeriac in this recipe. Onion seeds deserve to be used more – they add so much flavour to a dish. HP Sauce makes a tangy gravy to serve alongside. Select potatoes that are floury, so they crisp up nicely when cooked, such as Maris Piper.

Serves 4

2 large floury potatoes, peeled and grated

250g celeriac, peeled (100g finely grated, 150g roughly diced)

½ onion, peeled and finely grated

1 teaspoon table salt

70g non-dairy butter

100ml non-dairy milk

1 tablespoon onion seeds

¼ bunch of thyme, leaves picked

freshly milled black pepper

2 tablespoons vegetable oil

For the gravy

250ml Roasted Vegetable Stock (see page 180)

3 tablespoons HP Sauce

Put the potato, grated celeriac and onion in a large bowl. Mix in the salt and leave to sit for 10 minutes.

While the mix is salting, heat 30g of the butter in a medium saucepan. Add the diced celeriac to the pan and season well. Cook over a moderate–high heat until the celeriac is a dark golden colour and cooked through. Add the milk and cook for a further 3 minutes. Transfer the mix to a blender and blitz to a smooth purée. Keep warm.

Transfer the salted mix to a colander set over a bowl and press down to remove as much liquid as possible. Tip the grated veg onto a clean tea towel, wrap well and squeeze to remove all the liquid. Put the veg in a large bowl and add the onion seeds, thyme and black pepper.

Divide the rosti mix into 4 equal portions. Using 4 blini pans, or 2 large frying pans, heat the oil and remaining butter over a moderate–high heat. Press the mix into the blini pans, or shape into round patties, and fry for 4–5 minutes until golden. Gently flip over and cook the other side until golden.

For the gravy, pour the stock into a medium saucepan over a high heat. Bring to the boil and reduce until one-third remains. Whisk in the HP Sauce.

Serve the rostis with the caramelised celeriac purée and the HP gravy. Garnish the purée with onion seeds and thyme leaves.

Sweet Potato Fritters
with Avocado and Onion Jam

This is a winter comfort breakfast at its best. Don't be tempted to overmix the batter, otherwise the gluten in the flour will develop and your fritters will be rubbery rather than light and fluffy.

Serves 4/makes 12 fritters

2 large sweet potatoes, peeled and finely grated
1 teaspoon table salt
100g plain flour
1 teaspoon baking powder
100ml non-dairy milk
1 tablespoon finely chopped tarragon
½ green chilli, deseeded and finely diced
sea salt and freshly milled black pepper
3 tablespoons vegetable oil

zest and juice of 1 lime
1 teaspoon sriracha sauce
1 tablespoon olive oil
2 avocados
sea salt and freshly milled black pepper

4 tablespoons Onion Jam (see page 184)

Put the grated sweet potatoes in a large bowl with the salt and mix well. Leave to sit for 10 minutes, then tip into a colander set over a large bowl. Press to remove as much liquid as possible.

Put the flour and baking powder in a large bowl and mix well. Put the sweet potato, milk, tarragon and green chilli in a separate bowl, mix well, then add to the flour, with a good dose of black pepper. Gently mix to just combine.

Heat 2 tablespoons of the vegetable oil in a large frying pan over a moderate heat. When the oil is hot, drop 3 large spoonfuls of the batter into the pan, to form 3 fritters. Cook for 4–5 minutes until golden, then gently flip and cook the other side until golden. When cooked through, remove and set aside somewhere warm. Repeat with the remaining oil and batter.

Make a dressing by mixing the lime zest and juice, sriracha sauce and olive oil together. Halve, stone and slice the avocados and drizzle with the dressing. Season well.

To serve, place 3 fritters on each plate with half an avocado per serving and 1 tablespoon of onion jam.

Apple, Fennel and Fig Bircher Muesli

Bircher muesli does make mornings better, and more efficient! With your breakfast ready prepared in the fridge, you can just grab and go. Figs, fresh or dried, work well with it too; they are so sweet that there's no need for additional sugars. I like to use a mixture of jumbo oats and rolled oats, for added texture. The fennel, which may seem an unusual addition, adds a subtle licorice taste and a lovely crunch.

Serves 4

80g rolled oats

40g jumbo oats

2 tablespoons wheatgerm

25g almonds, toasted
and roughly chopped

25g hazelnuts, toasted
and roughly chopped

240ml non-dairy milk

1 apple, grated

¼ fennel bulb, grated

zest of 1 lime

4 figs, cut into 8 pieces each

Mix all the ingredients together and place in a container. Cover and refrigerate for at least 7 hours. The muesli will keep for 24 hours.

Caramelised Banana French Toast,
Maple and Smoked Sea Salt

French toast was one of my favourite foods when I was little. I loved the slightly gooey centre with the crisp, lightly salted outer layer. Lashings of maple syrup was always part of the drill too. Here, serving the toast with smoked sea salt balances out the sweetness.

Serves 4

8 x 2cm thick slices of Brioche (see page 167)

For the caramelised bananas

100g caster sugar

50g non-dairy butter

2 overripe medium bananas, peeled and roughly chopped

½ teaspoon ground cinnamon

pinch of table salt

150ml non-dairy milk

150ml oat cream

2 tablespoons soft dark brown sugar

25g non-dairy butter, for frying

2 bananas, each cut in half lenthways, then widthways, to form 8 pieces in total

To serve

maple syrup

smoked sea salt

Begin by making the caramelised bananas. Put the sugar in a medium heavy-based saucepan over a moderately high heat. Gently shake the pan when the sugar begins to melt. Do not stir, as this may cause the caramel to crystallise. As it keeps melting, keep shaking and swirling the pan until a medium-coloured caramel is formed. Turn down the heat, add the butter and whisk well. When fully combined, add the chopped bananas, cinnamon and salt. Cook, stirring regularly, over a low heat for 10–12 minutes until a thick purée is formed.

Put the milk, oat cream and sugar into a bowl and mix with a stick blender until the sugar has dissolved. Pour into a rectangular deep dish that will accommodate four brioche slices in a single layer.

Spread the banana purée over half the slices of brioche and top with the remaining slices. Place the brioche sandwiches into the cream mix and spoon the mix over the top of the bread. Allow to soak on both sides for 10 minutes until the liquid has been absorbed to the centre of the bread.

Melt half the butter in a large frying pan over a high heat. When hot, fry the sandwiches, in batches, until both sides are golden. Keep warm.

Using the same frying pan, add the remaining butter. When hot, add the banana slices and cook on both sides until golden.

Serve the brioche and banana slices with maple syrup and sea salt.

Mushroom, Spinach and Truffle Toast

Truffles have such a heady, fragranced flavour that is deep and rich in umami. I find some oils have a synthetic taste to them, so I always prefer to use truffle paste instead. It is not as intense, but it gives more of a true truffle flavour, with a wonderful heady aroma that oil sometimes misses. A little goes a long way, so keep a small jar in the fridge as it has a great shelf life. If you are not a fan, you can omit the truffle all together from the recipe.

Serves 4

15g dried porcini mushrooms
25g non-dairy butter
1 garlic clove, peeled and bashed
1 onion, peeled and finely sliced
25ml Madeira
100ml oat cream
¼ bunch of thyme, leaves picked
1 tablespoon truffle paste (optional)
sea salt and freshly milled black pepper

2 tablespoons vegetable oil
320g mixed mushrooms, washed
100g baby spinach
¼ bunch of tarragon, leaves picked and finely chopped

8 slices of sourdough bread

Put the porcini mushrooms in a small saucepan with 200ml water. Bring to the boil and simmer for 15 minutes. Remove from the heat and allow to sit for a further 30 minutes.

Heat the butter in a deep frying pan over a moderate heat. When hot, add the garlic and onion and season well. Cook until soft and lightly coloured. Add the Madeira and cook for a further 5 minutes. Add the rehydrated porcini mushrooms, with their soaking liquor, and simmer for 1 minute. Add the oat cream and thyme and simmer for 1 minute. Finish with the truffle paste, if using, and blend using a stick blender until a chunky purée is formed. Season to taste with salt and black pepper. Keep warm.

Heat the vegetable oil in a separate large frying pan. Fry the mixed mushrooms, seasoning well and working in batches so they colour rather than stew in an overcrowded pan. Once cooked, return the frying pan to the heat and when hot, add the spinach to quickly wilt.

Gently stir the tarragon through the mushrooms. Toast the sourdough, spread with the purée and top with the spinach and mushrooms.

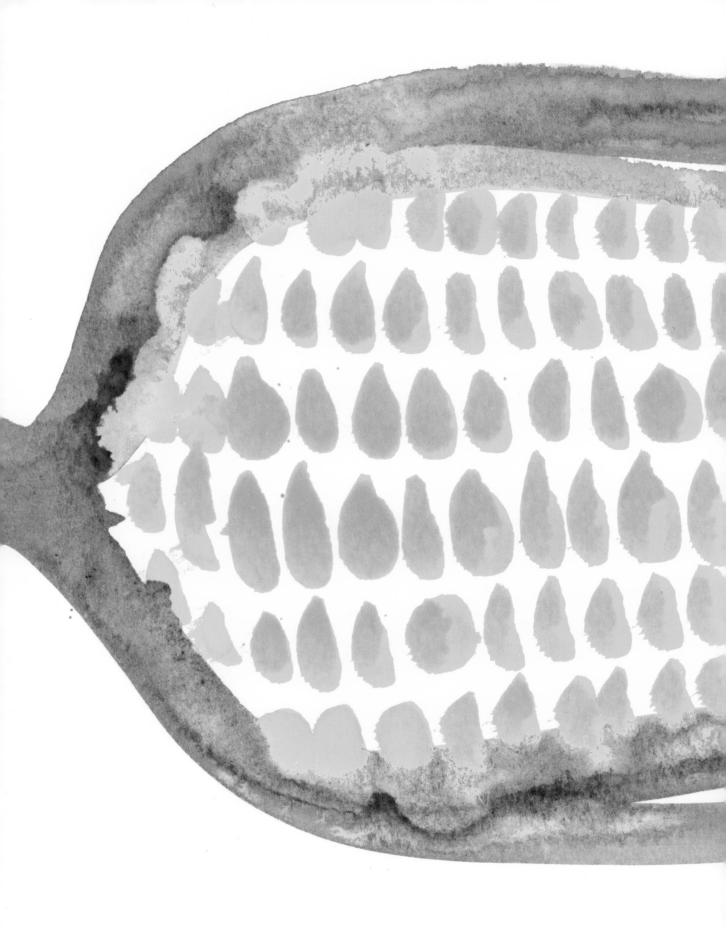

Snacks & Starters

Tequila-macerated Watermelon,

Pickled Rind, Kalamata Olives and Dukkah

Tequila is a wonderful spirit to use in cooking as it has so much flavour. For the maximum effect, macerate the watermelon in the tequila for 24 hours. This recipe uses the melon rind to make a fantastic pickle accompaniment to serve in salads, sandwiches or wraps. And the tequila left from macerating the watermelon makes a wonderful margarita...

Serves 6–8

½ small watermelon
100ml white wine vinegar
2 tablespoons agave syrup
8 white peppercorns
2 cloves
1 bay leaf
1cm knob of ginger, peeled
½ teaspoon yellow mustard seeds
½ teaspoon table salt
100ml tequila
1 quantity of Dukkah
80g Kalamata olives, halved and pitted
micro coriander, to garnish

Peel the green rind off the watermelon then carefully slice the white flesh off the pink flesh. Cut the white flesh into roughly 1cm chunks. Put the vinegar, agave, peppercorns, cloves, bay leaf, ginger, yellow mustard seeds and salt into a small saucepan and bring to the boil. Add the watermelon rind and bring back up to the boil. Remove from the heat and allow to steep for 30 minutes. Cover and refrigerate for at least 24 hours.

Dice the pink watermelon flesh into roughly 3cm cubes. Put in a shallow container and pour the tequila over the top. Cover and refrigerate for at least 24 hours, gently shaking a few times to ensure all the cubes are covered.

Strain off the watermelon cubes and lay on a tray.

Dip each watermelon cube into the dukkah so that half the cube is coated. Top with a slice of watermelon rind and an olive half. Garnish with the micro coriander and serve.

Dukkah

Makes about 160g

50g hazelnuts
50g almonds
10g black sesame seeds
10g white sesame seeds
1 tablespoon coriander seeds
1 tablespoon cumin seeds
1 teaspoon fennel seeds
1 teaspoon flaked sea salt
½ teaspoon freshly milled black pepper

Preheat the oven to 180°C/fan 160°C/gas mark 4.

Put all the ingredients into a roasting tin. Bake for 8–10 minutes until fragrant, then pulse in a blender to a crumb-like consistency.

Sweetcorn Fritters
with Chipotle Mojo Sauce

Sweetcorn fritters were somewhat of a staple go-to food when I was growing up. They made a great weekend breakfast, winter lunch or lazy supper. They work well with lashings of avocado and chilli sauce for brunch or make good snacks or canapés. They are generally a hit with the kids too. Chipotle is a smoke-dried jalapeño pepper which has a lovely, rich smoky flavour and pairs perfectly with these fritters.

Serves 8

200g plain flour
10g baking powder
1 x 198g can sweetcorn
130g aquafaba
1 tablespoon chopped coriander leaves
sea salt and freshly milled black pepper
4 tablespoons vegetable oil

1 quantity Chipotle Mojo Sauce, to serve

In a bowl, mix the flour and baking powder together. Make a well in the centre and add the whole can of sweetcorn, liquid included, the aquafaba, coriander and a generous twist of black pepper. Gently mix until just combined, taking care not to overmix, otherwise the fritters will be rubbery, not fluffy. Check the seasoning, adding a little more if needed.

Heat half the oil in a large non-stick frying pan, and add 6–8 individual teaspoonfuls of the fritter batter. Brown on one side, then gently flip over and brown the other side. Cook for 3–4 minutes in total until the batter is cooked through. Fry in batches, adding more oil when necessary, then drain on kitchen paper to remove any excess oil.

Serve the hot fritters with the Chipotle Mojo Sauce.

Chipotle Mojo Sauce

50g piquillo peppers (from a can or jar), drained weight
½ yellow pepper, deseeded
50g flaked almonds, toasted
50g olive oil
1 tablespoon finely chopped coriander
1 teaspoon chipotle paste
zest and juice of ½ lime
sea salt and freshly milled black pepper

Put all the ingredients in a blender and blend to a smooth paste is formed. Adjust the seasoning if necessary.

Kimchi Pancakes

This is a combination of two of my favourite things – kimchi and pancakes! They make a good snack, and also can be adapted for canapés if you make smaller ones. Try serving them with a little coconut yogurt mixed with some mango chutney and coriander. You can also keep the batter in the fridge overnight and use it on two consecutive days.

Serves 4

100g plain flour
¼ teaspoon sweet smoked paprika
½ teaspoon baking powder
40g rice flour
½ teaspoon table salt
180g Kimchi, finely chopped
40ml Kimchi liquid
1 tablespoon finely chopped coriander leaves
2 tablespoons vegetable oil

In a bowl, mix the flour, paprika, baking powder, rice flour and salt together. Make a well in the centre, add the kimchi, kimchi liquid, 50ml water and the coriander. Gently mix together until smooth, taking care not to overmix to ensure the pancakes are light and fluffy.

Heat a little of the oil in a large non-stick frying pan over a medium–high heat. Drop teaspoonfuls of the pancake batter into the oil and cook for 2 minutes, or until golden-brown underneath and bubbles appear on the top of the pancake. Gently flip over and cook for a further 1–2 minutes. Remove from the pan and drain on kitchen paper. Repeat with the remaining batter, adding more oil when needed.

Kimchi

Makes one large jar (1.5 litres)

For the paste
2 garlic cloves, bashed and peeled
a large knob (15cm) ginger, peeled and finely grated
2 tablespoons palm sugar, grated
2 tablespoons Korean red pepper powder, or Gochujang if unavailable
3 tablespoons rice wine vinegar
1 tablespoon table salt

1 Chinese cabbage, core removed, finely chopped
1 mooli, peeled and finely sliced
1 fennel bulb, finely sliced

Put all the ingredients for the paste into a blender and blend to a smooth paste.

Using disposable gloves, massage the paste into the cabbage, mooli and fennel for 10 minutes.

Pack the kimchi into a large, clean jar. Cover the top with clingfilm and leave at room temperature for 3 days, then cover with a lid and refrigerate. It will keep for up to 3 months refrigerated.

Fermented Mushroom Pâté
with Lapsang Souchong Jelly

Fermenting enhances the savouriness and overall flavour of ingredients. In this recipe, the fermentation intensifies the umami flavour in the mushrooms, creating a rich and delicious pâté. The wonderful smokiness of lapsang souchong tea makes this a great combo. I serve it with seeded crackers or a good sourdough, sliced and toasted. Note that the best flavour will come from a three-day fermentation, so you will need to plan ahead to make this.

Serves 4

For the mushroom pâté

250g chestnut mushrooms, finely sliced

300g flat cap mushrooms, finely sliced

2 banana shallots, peeled and finely sliced

2 garlic cloves, peeled and finely grated

½ bunch thyme, plus an extra sprig for garnishing

50ml olive oil

100ml non-dairy milk

25ml Madeira

1 teaspoon table salt

freshly milled black pepper

50g non-dairy butter

For the lapsang souchong jelly

1 tablespoon lapsang souchong tea

½ 6.5g sachet Vege-Gel (vegan gelatine)

25ml Madeira

3 teaspoons maple syrup

Put all the ingredients for the mushroom pâté into a large mixing bowl. Using your hands, mix everything together and massage the mushrooms so they begin to break down.

Pack the mixture tightly into a clean 1-litre jar. Cover with clingfilm and leave at room temperature for 3 days.

Pour the contents of the jar into a colander set over a bowl. Allow the majority of the liquid to drain off, reserving the liquid in the bowl, and set aside.

Heat the butter in a large saucepan over a medium–high heat. Add the contents of the colander. Cook the mushrooms for 10 minutes until most of the excess liquid has evaporated. Add the reserved liquid from the fermentation and cook for a further 10 minutes.

Remove the thyme sprigs, then tip the contents of the pan into a blender. Blend until smooth and transfer to a dish, approximately 19 x 12cm. Using the back of a spoon or a knife, smooth the top and refrigerate for 2 hours.

For the jelly, bring 250ml water to the boil. Add the tea and Vege-Gel, whisk well and leave to sit for 6 minutes. Whisk well again then strain through a fine-mesh sieve. Stir in the Madeira and maple syrup.

Remove the pâté from the fridge and carefully pour over the jelly. Pick the leaves from the reserved thyme sprig and sprinkle on top of the jelly. Refrigerate for a further 2 hours, then serve.

Crispy Sage Leaves and Sweet Potato Skins with Smoked Paprika Rouille

Crispy sage leaves are one of the simplest, yet delicious, snacks. They are also great as a garnish in salads, pastas, pizzas and soups. Select sage leaves that are large and upright. To store bunches in the fridge, dampen some kitchen paper and wrap it around the base of the stalks, then cover the entire bunch with clingfilm. This will prolong the life of any herbs and protect them from bruising. Rouille is traditionally a thick, garlicky mayonnaise. Here, I use sweet potato as the main thickener, and their skins as tasty crisps for dunking.

Serves 8

For the rouille

2 small sweet potatoes

2 tablespoons Roast Garlic Purée (see page 185)

40g aquafaba

zest and juice of ¼ lemon

¼ red chilli, finely diced

1½ teaspoons sweet smoked paprika

sea salt and freshly milled black pepper

150ml olive oil

vegetable oil, for frying

20–24 large sage leaves

1 quantity of Tempura Batter (see page 180)

Preheat the oven to 180°C/fan 160°C/gas mark 4.

Prick the sweet potatoes with a fork, place on a baking tray and bake for 15–20 minutes until completely soft. Remove from the oven, slice in half lengthways and allow to sit for 20 minutes for the steam to escape.

Scoop out the flesh of the sweet potatoes. Cut the skins into pieces roughly the size of the sage leaves and reserve.

Put the sweet potato flesh in a blender (or a beaker if using a stick blender) and add the garlic purée, aquafaba, lemon zest and juice, red chilli, sweet smoked paprika and a good twist of black pepper. Blend together until smooth, then slowly drizzle in the olive oil, blending well after each addition. Season with salt and set aside.

Heat the vegetable oil in a deep-fat fryer, or pour enough oil into a medium saucepan to reach 3cm in depth to 170°C. Dip each sage leaf in the tempura batter and carefully drop a few at a time in the hot oil. Fry for 1–2 minutes until crispy, then remove with a slotted spoon, drain on kitchen paper and season with salt. Repeat with all the sage leaves, and then the sweet potato skins. Work in batches until all the leaves and skins are cooked.

Serve the sage leaves and sweet potato skins while hot, with the rouille.

Parsnip and Horseradish Pâté
with Flatbread Crisps

Parsnip and horseradish are a rather magical combination and it has been one of my favourites for years. I first began making a version of this pâté just before I moved to London – so, many moons ago! Fresh horseradish looks a bit like a long parsnip. It lasts for quite some time in the fridge and works well grated over any dish to add a slight kick.

Serves 4

For the horseradish pâté

3–5 parsnips (about 500g), peeled and diced into 4cm chunks

2 tablespoons vegetable oil

½ teaspoon table salt

freshly milled black pepper

½ horseradish root, peeled

100ml oat cream

For the flatbread crisps

2 flatbreads

1 tablespoon olive oil

1 teaspoon finely chopped rosemary

sea salt and freshly milled black pepper

Preheat the oven to 180°C/fan 160°C/gas mark 4. For the pâté, place the parsnip chunks in a roasting dish with the oil, salt and pepper. Bake for 20–25 minutes until golden. Remove from the oven and allow to cool for 10 minutes.

Put the cooled parsnips in a blender, or beaker if using a stick blender. Finely grate the horseradish into the parsnip. Add the oat cream and pulse until a chunky purée is formed. Adjust the seasoning if necessary and transfer to a small serving bowl.

To make the flatbread crisps, cut each flatbread into 8 wedges. Brush each liberally with the oil, then sprinkle generously with the rosemary, salt and black pepper. Bake for 6–8 minutes until lightly golden.

Serve the crisps with the pâté.

Wild Garlic 'Sushi Rolls'
with Brown Rice, Pickled Ginger and Soy Aïoli

For me, wild garlic signals the beginning of spring. Growing up in New Zealand, I recall the garlicky smell permeating the air on weekend mornings when the neighbours were mowing their lawns. At the time, I thought it rather unpleasant but now I absolutely love to include the more subtle flavour of wild garlic leaves in my food. Here, I have made what looks something like a sushi roll, which makes the perfect snack, canapé or light spring lunch.

Serves 4

½ quantity of Mustard Pickle (see page 185)

1 large knob of ginger, 10cm in length, peeled and finely sliced

160g brown rice

1 teaspoon soy sauce

1 garlic clove, peeled

2 tablespoons rice wine vinegar

1 tablespoon sesame oil

For the soy aïoli

1 quantity of Roast Garlic Aïoli (see page 184)

3 tablespoons soy sauce

½ teaspoon wasabi paste

½ teaspoon xanthan gum

24 large wild garlic leaves

Begin by pickling the ginger. Strain the hot mustard pickle through a sieve into a medium saucepan. Add the ginger and set the pan over a low heat for 20 minutes. Remove the pan from the heat and cover with clingfilm. Allow to sit for 2 hours, then refrigerate.

To cook the rice, rinse well, then place in medium saucepan. Cover with 250ml water and add the soy sauce and garlic. Bring to the boil then reduce the heat and cover with a lid. Simmer for 40 minutes, until all the water has absorbed. Remove from the heat and allow to sit, covered, for a further 10 minutes. Remove the garlic, stir in the rice wine vinegar and sesame oil, then transfer to a shallow casserole dish to cool. Refrigerate.

For the soy aïoli, make the Roast Garlic Aïoli. Whisk in the soy sauce and wasabi paste. Add the xanthan gum and whisk vigorously until the mix thickens. Transfer to a serving bowl, cover and refrigerate.

Lay a double layer of clingfilm on a work surface. Boil the kettle and pour the hot water into a shallow dish, large enough to fit a leaf of wild garlic. Season the water well with salt then place 4 leaves in the water for 10 seconds. Dry on kitchen paper then place, overlapping, on the clingfilm, to form a rectangle. Place one-sixth of the seasoned rice on the garlic leaves and smooth out, leaving a 2cm border all around. Place one-sixth of the ginger in the centre of the rice, then roll up the garlic over the rice, using the clingfilm to wrap. Roll into a tight sausage shape and tie the clingfilm at each end tightly. Refrigerate and repeat to make a further 5 rolls with the remaining ingredients.

Allow the sushi rolls to chill for at least 1 hour, then remove the clingfilm and slice into portions. Serve with the soy aïoli.

Tempura Spring Onions
with Romesco Sauce

I much prefer spring onions cooked to raw. Their wonderful sweetness only comes out when heat is applied, and they are delicious grilled, roasted or deep fried. Romesco sauce is a great go-to sauce to have to hand in your fridge: a combination of sweet piquillo peppers, almonds and parsley with a splash of sherry vinegar and lashings of olive oil. It transforms a meal and makes a great dip, sauce or salad dressing.

Serves 4

1 quantity of Romesco Sauce
1 quantity of Tempura Batter (see page 180)
vegetable oil, for deep frying
2 bunches of spring onions, roots cleaned
plain flour, for dusting
sea salt

Begin by making the Romesco Sauce, then the tempura batter.

Heat the oil in a deep-fat fryer, or pour enough oil into a medium saucepan to reach 3cm in depth, then heat to 170°C. Dust each spring onion with flour, then dip in the tempura batter and carefully drop in the hot oil, 3 at time. Fry for 2–3 minutes until crispy, then remove with a slotted spoon, drain on kitchen paper and season with salt. Repeat with the remaining spring onions.

Serve, while hot, with the Romesco sauce to dip.

Romesco Sauce

100g piquillo peppers (from a can or jar), drained weight
50g flaked almonds, toasted
40ml olive oil
½ teaspoon sweet smoked paprika
1 tablespoon finely chopped parsley
2 tablespoons tomato purée
1 teaspoon sherry vinegar
sea salt and freshly milled black pepper

Put all the ingredients in a blender and pulse until a chunky paste is formed. Adjust the seasoning if necessary.

Broad Bean 'Cacio e Pepe',
with Chargrilled Runner Beans and Confit Lemon

Cacio e pepe means 'cheese and pepper' in Italian and usually refers to a simple dish of spaghetti, pecorino cheese and black pepper. Here I'm using the same idea to cook broad beans, served with grilled runner beans and confit lemon.

Serves 4

200g podded broad beans
½ teaspoon freshly milled black pepper
25g vegan pecorino, finely grated
table salt

6 runner beans
1 tablespoon vegetable oil

8 slices of Confit Lemon

Bring a medium saucepan of salted water to the boil. Add the broad beans and blanch for 1 minute. Remove and refresh in cold water. Reserve 100ml of the blanching water. When the beans are cold, pop them out of their skins.

Put the black pepper in a medium frying pan over a moderate heat. Toast the pepper for a few minutes until fragrant. Add the broad beans and the reserved blanching water. Bring to the boil, then add the pecorino and stir vigorously until the cheese mixes with the water. Turn the heat down low.

Heat a griddle pan until almost smoking. Brush the runner beans with the oil. Season well, then grill on each side for 1–2 minutes until charred and a little soft.

Halve the beans and serve with the broad bean cacio e pepe and the confit lemon slices.

Confit Lemon

100g caster sugar
3 unwaxed lemons, finely sliced

Put the sugar in a saucepan with 400ml of water and bring to a simmer. When the sugar has dissolved, add the lemon slices and cook over a very low heat 1 an hour until the lemons become translucent. Cool then refrigerate for up to 2 months.

Grilled Asparagus,
Gremolata, Macadamia and Elderflower

Gremolata is a flavoursome condiment made with parsley, lemon zest and garlic. It adds a lovely burst of savouriness and is a useful go-to accompaniment for almost any dish. In spring, try adding a little wild garlic, which grows widely in areas that are a little damp and shaded.

Serves 4

2 bunches of asparagus

1 tablespoon vegetable oil

60g macadamia nuts, roughly chopped in half

¼ teaspoon fennel seeds

3 tablespoons olive oil

1 tablespoon elderflower cordial

2 slices of sourdough bread

sea salt and freshly milled black pepper

fresh elderflower heads, to garnish (optional)

For the gremolata

2 tablespoons finely chopped flat-leaf parsley

zest of 1 lemon

1 tablespoon finely chopped wild garlic leaves

1 garlic clove, peeled and finely grated

table salt

Preheat the oven to 180°C/fan 160°C/gas mark 4.

Gently snap off the woody ends of the asparagus – the spear will naturally snap at the point where the stalk becomes woody. Neaten the end of each spear with a knife. Bring a large saucepan of heavily salted water to the boil. Add the asparagus and blanch for 2 minutes, then refresh in cold water. Drain well and drizzle with the vegetable oil.

Put the macadamia nuts and fennel seeds on a baking tray and bake for 8–10 minutes until the nuts are golden. Remove from the oven and set aside.

For the gremolata, mix all the ingredients together and season to taste with salt.

Mix 2 tablespoons of the olive oil with the elderflower cordial and set aside.

Break the bread into bite-sized pieces and brush with the remaining olive oil.

Heat a griddle pan over a high heat until almost smoking. Season the asparagus spears with salt and black pepper. Grill, in batches, until charred on all sides. Chargrill the bread until golden.

Divide the asparagus and sourdough croutons between four plates. Drizzle with the elderflower dressing and top with the gremolata and macadamia crumb. Garnish with elderflower heads, if available.

Chargrilled Courgette Soup,
Spring Onion Bhajis

Chargrilling vegetables for soup is a great way to use up any vegetables that are about to go past their best. They take on a wonderfully smoky flavour that makes the soup even more satisfying and delicious. I love bhajis so, paired with the soup, this is a winning combination for me.

Serves 4

For the soup

4 tablespoons vegetable oil

1 onion, peeled and finely sliced

¼ teaspoon cumin seeds

2 garlic cloves, crushed

8 courgettes, halved lengthways

½ bunch of tarragon, leaves stripped

1 litre Roast Vegetable Stock (see page 180)

200g baby spinach

table salt and freshly milled black pepper

For the bhajis

1 bunch of spring onions, finely sliced

1 onion, peeled and finely sliced

1cm knob of turmeric, peeled and finely grated

½ teaspoon cumin seeds, toasted

1 tablespoon finely chopped coriander

½ teaspoon finely chopped green chilli, seeds discarded

3 tablespoons chickpea flour

25g aquafaba

vegetable oil, for deep frying

avocado oil, for drizzling

Start by making the soup. Put 2 tablespoons of the oil in a medium saucepan over a moderate to high heat. When hot, add the onion, cumin seeds and garlic and cook until soft, but not coloured.

Meanwhile, place a griddle pan over a high heat. Drizzle the courgette halves with the remaining oil and season well. Grill on each side until well charred, then add to the saucepan. Add the tarragon, stock and a good grinding of black pepper. Simmer over a low heat for 10 minutes until the courgettes are soft. Add the spinach, cook for a further minute, then blend the soup until smooth. Adjust the seasoning if necessary. Keep warm.

For the bhajis, mix together all the ingredients, except the aquafaba. When combined, add the aquafaba, season well and mix until a sticky batter is formed. Fill a medium saucepan one-third full with vegetable oil and heat to 160°C. Fry tablespoonfuls of the bhaji mix in the oil for about 4 minutes, until golden and cooked through. The mix will make 8 bhajis. Drain on kitchen paper.

Drizzle a little avocado oil on top of each bowl of soup before serving with the bhajis.

Kohlrabi Ravioli
Pea and Avocado Guacamole, Avocado Oil Aïoli, Lemon Jam

This is a super-fresh dish whereby thinly sliced kohlrabi is used instead of pasta. It creates a deliciously crunchy wrapper for the creamy guacamole. This makes an interesting and tasty starter.

Serves 4

2 large kohlrabi, peeled
1 teaspoon rice wine vinegar
1 teaspoon avocado oil

For the pea guacamole

1 avocado, halved, stoned and peeled
8 mint leaves, finely chopped
8 coriander leaves, finely chopped
100g frozen peas, defrosted
1 shallot, peeled and finely diced
zest and juice of ½ lime
¼ teaspoon wasabi paste
sea salt and freshly milled black pepper

For the avocado oil aïoli

30g aquafaba
½ teaspoon Dijon mustard
1 garlic clove, peeled and finely grated
1 teaspoon rice wine vinegar
40ml olive oil
50ml avocado oil
½ teaspoon table salt

2 teaspoons Baked Citrus Jam

To serve
pea shoots
edible flowers

Using a mandoline, thinly slice the kohlrabi into rounds about 2mm thick. You should have 24 rounds in total. Whisk the rice wine vinegar and avocado oil together to make a vinaigrette.

For the guacamole, put all the ingredients into a blender and pulse until a semi-smooth purée is formed. Season to taste.

For the avocado oil aïoli, whisk the aquafaba, mustard, garlic and rice wine together until combined. Slowly drizzle in the oils, whisking continuously until fully incorporated. Season to taste.

To assemble, brush half the kohlrabi rounds with the vinaigrette. Place 1 teaspoonful of the guacamole in the centre of each round then top with another round of kohlrabi. Gently press on the edges of the rounds to seal the 'raviolis'.

Divide the raviolis between 4 serving bowls and season with salt and black pepper. Garnish with pea shoots and edible flowers and serve with the aïoli and citrus jam.

Baked Citrus Jam

2 lemons (or equivalent approximate weight of other citrus fruit)
4 tablespoons caster sugar
2 tablespoons olive oil
pinch of sea salt

Preheat the oven to 200°C/fan 180°C/gas mark 6.

Put the whole fruit on a foil-lined baking sheet or roasting dish. Bake for 40 minutes until golden and soft. Allow to cool, then blend with the sugar, oil, salt and 25ml of water. Add more water if necessary to form a thick 'jam'.

Chilled Sweetcorn Soup,
Chargrilled Sweetcorn, Pickled Onion and Tarragon

Sweetcorn is one of my favourite vegetables and I always look forward to it coming into season. Look for corn cobs that are vibrant and firm, with the outer husks not wilting or browning. Peel a small part of the husks back to check that the kernels are bright yellow. Always keep the cobs too as they make for a sweet stock.

Serves 4

2 corn on the cob

1 tablespoon vegetable oil

sea salt and freshly milled black pepper

For the soup

4 corn on the cob, kernels sliced off and cobs retained

1 onion, peeled and quartered

2 bay leaves

1 garlic clove, peeled

½ teaspoon coriander seeds

1 bunch of tarragon, leaves picked and chopped, and stalks reserved for the pickle

3 tablespoons non-dairy butter

1 teaspoon table salt

100ml coconut milk

For the pickled onion and tarragon

2 tablespoons vegetable oil

2 red onions, peeled and finely sliced

2 garlic cloves, peeled and finely grated

½ red chilli, finely diced

50ml red wine vinegar

Heat a griddle pan until almost smoking or fire up the barbecue until very hot. Brush the 2 sweetcorn cobs with the oil and season well. Grill for 4–6 minutes until charred on the outside and cooked through. Remove from the heat, cover in foil and leave to sit for 10 minutes. Slice the kernels off the cobs by standing the cobs on their end and cutting downwards, then set aside.

Put the 2 trimmed cobs from the chargrilled corn into a large saucepan with the other 4 trimmed cobs, saving the kernels for later. Add the onion, bay leaves, garlic, coriander seeds and the stalks of the tarragon. Cover with water and set the pan over a high heat. Bring to the boil, then simmer for 30 minutes. Strain off, discarding all but the stock.

Heat the butter in a large saucepan over a high heat. When melted, add the raw sweetcorn kernels and salt and cook for about 10 minutes, until soft. Add three-quarters of the stock and bring to a simmer. Simmer gently for 20 minutes, then remove from the heat. Add the coconut milk and blend until smooth, adding more of the stock if necessary, remembering that the consistency will thicken when chilled. Pour into a large container, cover the surface of the soup with clingfilm and place in the fridge to chill, whisking regularly.

For the pickled onion and tarragon, heat the oil in a medium frying pan over a moderate heat. When hot, add the red onions and season well. Cook, stirring frequently, for 15–20 minutes until the onions start to caramelise. Add the garlic and chilli and cook for a further 5 minutes. Add the red wine vinegar and cook for a further 5 minutes. Remove from the heat and set aside to cool. When cooled, add the tarragon leaves and mix well.

To serve, divide the pickled onion mix between four bowls. Add the chargrilled corn kernels, pour the chilled soup over the top and serve.

Spring Salad:
Wild Garlic Tahini, Grilled Spring Onions, Pea and Broad Bean Salsa, Sorrel, Pickled Onion with Lemon Confit

This salad really epitomises the freshness and newness of spring, with a nice kick of wild garlic! Peas and broad beans feature heavily, but feel free to add or substitute any other vegetables you have available. I really enjoy adding different herbs to tahini; it adds a vibrancy and freshness that works well in salads and as a garnish for most dishes.

Serves 4

1 red onion, peeled and finely sliced

100ml Mustard Pickle (see page 185)

1 bunch of spring onions

1 tablespoon vegetable oil

For the wild garlic tahini

50g wild garlic leaves

50g toasted sesame seeds

2 tablespoons sesame oil

½ teaspoon agave syrup

50ml olive oil

juice of 1 lemon

sea salt and freshly milled black pepper

For the salsa

1 tablespoon vegetable oil

2 shallots, peeled and finely diced

½ red chilli, deseeded and finely chopped

100g podded fresh peas

100g podded broad beans

To serve

1 handful of sorrel leaves

2 tablespoons of Confit Lemon (see page 39)

Put the red onion in a small bowl. Bring the mustard pickle to a gentle simmer, then pour over the onion and refrigerate.

For the tahini, put all the ingredients in a blender with 50ml of cold water. Blend until a paste is formed and season to taste, adding more water if needed.

To make the salsa, heat the oil in a small frying pan, then add the shallots and chilli. Season well, then cook until the shallots are soft but not coloured. Add the peas and broad beans and cook for 2 minutes. Transfer to a large bowl and use a stick blender to pulse until a chunky salsa is formed.

Heat a griddle pan until almost smoking. Brush the spring onions with the oil, season well and grill until charred.

To assemble, add a good dollop of the tahini to 4 bowls. Top with the grilled spring onions and the pea and broad bean salsa. Serve with the sorrel leaves, lemon confit and finish with the pickled red onion.

Heirloom Tomatoes,
Pan Con Tomate, Basil

This version of *pan con tomate* is more of a tomato and garlic-infused
French toast than the much-loved Spanish classic. While this makes a good
starter or lunchtime dish, it's also a great brunch.

Serves 4

250ml tomato juice

50g aquafaba

dash of Tabasco

1 garlic clove, peeled and finely grated

4 slices of sourdough bread

1 tablespoon non-dairy butter

50ml extra virgin olive oil

1 garlic clove, peeled

1 teaspoon balsamic vinegar

400g heirloom tomatoes, sliced into
wedges or 1cm slices

sea salt and freshly milled black pepper

micro basil cress, to garnish (optional)

Whisk together the tomato juice, aquafaba, Tabasco, garlic, salt and
black pepper and pour into a shallow dish large enough to fit the sourdough
slices side by side. Place the bread in the liquid and leave for 10 minutes.
Gently turn over and leave for a further 10 minutes until all the liquid has
been absorbed.

Heat the butter in a large frying pan over a moderately high heat. When hot,
add the soaked sourdough and colour well on both sides.

Put the oil, garlic and balsamic vinegar in a bowl. Season with salt and mix
well. Place the tomatoes in the bowl and toss to coat, seasoning well with
salt and black pepper.

Serve the toast with the tomatoes on top and garnish with the micro basil.

Cucumber Granita,
Pickled Cucumber, Basil, Chilli, Avocado and Crispy Onion Rings

This dish is the ultimate summer cooler. It may sound rather different from a usual starter, but do try it – it's cool, creamy and a little spicy. It is a great way to use up any cucumbers that are almost past their best, too. The tequila adds a lovely smokiness to the granita, but if you are not a fan you can substitute with vodka or gin.

Serves 4

For the cucumber granita

2 cucumbers, roughly chopped

25ml white wine vinegar

1 teaspoon table salt

zest and juice of 1 lime

1 tablespoon agave syrup

50ml tequila

For the pickled cucumber

½ cucumber

200ml Mustard Pickle (see page 185)

1 avocado, halved, stoned and peeled

½ red chilli, finely sliced

½ bunch of basil, leaves chopped

2 tablespoons olive oil

1 teaspoon white wine vinegar

vegetable oil, for frying

1 teaspoon onion seeds

1 quantity of Tempura Batter (see page 180)

2 onions, peeled and sliced into 1cm rounds

flour, for dusting

Blend all the ingredients for the granita in batches to a smooth purée. Adjust the seasoning if necessary, then pour into a freezerproof container and put in the freezer. Whisk every 30 minutes until frozen solid.

To make the pickled cucumber, slice the ½ cucumber into 3mm rounds. Put the mustard pickle in a small saucepan and bring to a simmer. Pour over the cucumber and refrigerate.

Slice the avocado into 5mm slices. Put in a bowl with the chilli and basil leaves. Mix the olive oil and white wine vinegar together, then pour over the avocado. Season well with salt.

Heat a deep-fat fryer to 160°C, or pour enough vegetable oil in a medium saucepan to fill by one-third, and heat to 160°C. Mix the onion seeds into the tempura batter. Dust the onion rounds in the flour, then coat in the tempura batter. Fry, in batches, until golden. Carefully remove the onion rings with a slotted spoon and drain on kitchen paper.

To assemble, use a fork to flake the granita and share between 4 bowls. Top with the pickled cucumber slices, avocado and finish with the crispy onion rings.

Caramelised Aubergine Tartlet,
Zhoug, Coconut and Coriander

Zhoug has its origins in Yemeni cuisine. It can be quite spicy, but the additional herbs and spices in the recipe make this one of my favourite accompaniments. It pairs really well with the unctuous, savoury aubergine. Pomegranate molasses is one of my favourite ingredients too; it has a rich sweetness that is so well balanced with a rounded acidity.

Serves 4

2 aubergines
50ml vegetable oil
1 teaspoon table salt

1 quantity of Zhoug (see page 181)

½ teaspoon cumin seeds
4 sheets of filo pastry
2 tablespoons olive oil

100g coconut yogurt
½ bunch of coriander, leaves chopped
2 tablespoons pomegranate molasses
micro coriander, to garnish (optional)

Preheat the oven to 180°C/fan 160°C/gas mark 4.

Peel one of the aubergines and dice into 2cm chunks. Heat half the vegetable oil in a large saucepan over a medium–high heat. When hot, add the aubergine and salt and cook for 15–20 minutes, stirring frequently, until a deep golden colour. Once cooked, set aside.

Halve the other aubergine lengthways, and cut into 5mm slices. Salt each slice and leave for 10 minutes. Rinse the salt off and pat dry with kitchen paper.

Meanwhile make the zhoug.

Toast the cumin seeds in a dry frying pan over a moderate heat until fragrant. Remove the seeds from the pan and crush, using a mortar and pestle or spice grinder.

Lay a sheet of filo pastry on your worktop. Brush liberally with olive oil. Add another sheet of pastry on top and brush liberally with olive oil again. Sprinkle the crushed cumin seeds over the top. Layer the last two sheets of filo on top, brushing with olive oil. Slice the pastry into eight even pieces, then place between two sheets of parchment paper. Slide onto a baking tray and place another tray on top to sandwich the pastry together. Bake for 10–12 minutes until the pastry sheets are golden.

Heat a griddle pan until hot. Brush the aubergine slices with the remaining oil and grill each side until nicely charred.

Mix the yogurt with the coriander and pomegranate molasses.

Divide the aubergines between the eight sheets of filo. Place one rectangle on top of another and drizzle the top with the zhoug and yogurt. Garnish with the micro coriander, if using, and serve.

Summer Salad:
Apricot and Green Chilli Mole, Charred Sugar Snap Peas, Courgettes and Garden Leaves

When the weather is hot all I crave is flavoursome salads. This one ticks all the boxes and the apricot and green chilli mole brings a sweet and spicy dimension to it that works super well. Feel free to substitute any fresh vegetables you have in the salad, and if you cannot get ripe apricots this also works really well with nectarines or peaches.

Serves 4

For the apricot and green chilli mole

1 green chilli, finely chopped

½ bunch of coriander

½ bunch of basil

1 garlic clove, peeled and finely grated

½ teaspoon cumin seeds

2 cloves, finely crushed

50g flaked almonds

zest and juice of 1 lime

50ml olive oil

2 apricots, halved, stoned and roughly chopped

sea salt and freshly milled black pepper

200g sugar snap peas

2 tablespoons olive oil

2 courgettes, finely sliced

4 tablespoons Basic Vinaigrette (see page 186)

200g mixed salad leaves

8–12 edible flowers (optional)

For the mole, put the chilli, herbs, garlic, spices, almonds and lime zest and juice into a blender and blitz to a paste. Add the oil and blend together. Add the apricots, season well and blend until a thick paste is formed.

Heat a griddle pan or the barbecue. Toss the sugar snap peas in the oil and season well with salt and black pepper. When the griddle is almost smoking, chargrill the sugar snap peas in batches until well charred but still crunchy.

Put the courgettes into a bowl and season well. Add half the vinaigrette and mix well.

Put the salad leaves in a large bowl with the remaining vinaigrette. Season and mix well.

To assemble the salad, spoon the mole into the centre of a large bowl and, using a spoon, smear around the outside. Place the peas on top, followed by the salad leaves. Finish with the courgettes and garnish with edible flowers, if using.

Autumn Salad:

Crispy Brussel Sprouts, Butternut Squash, Kale Salsa

Whenever people tell me that they dislike Brussels sprouts, I want to say that they've just not had them cooked properly! Sprouts have such a wonderful nutty flavour that is simply delicious. I like them crispy on the outside and al dente in the centre. This recipe also calls for 'massaging' the raw kale. This may sound odd, but do try it, as it really enhances the flavour.

Serves 4

1 butternut squash
1 teaspoon onion seeds
3 tablespoons vegetable oil
100ml Mustard Pickle (see page 185)
200g Brussels sprouts, halved
2 tablespoons sunflower spread
200g kale
sea salt and freshly milled black pepper

For the kale salsa

100g kale
zest and juice of 1 lime
50ml olive oil
1 garlic clove, peeled and finely grated
½ teaspoon Dijon mustard
1 tablespoon capers
1 tablespoon chopped flat-leaf parsley
1 tablespoon chopped tarragon leaves

Preheat the oven to 180°C/fan 160°C/gas mark 4. Peel the butternut squash, halve lengthways and remove the seeds using a spoon. Slice into 6 wedges. Set one of the wedges aside and slice the other 5 in half lengthways. Mix the onion seeds with half the vegetable oil, and toss the small squash wedges in the oil. Season well with salt and black pepper, then place on a baking sheet or roasting tray. Roast for 15–20 minutes until golden. Peel the remaining large squash wedge into ribbons and submerge in the mustard pickle.

For the kale salsa, put the kale in a blender jug. Add the lime zest and juice, olive oil, garlic, mustard, capers, parsley and tarragon and blitz to a paste. Add 50–100ml of water – enough to make a runny salsa. Season to taste and set aside.

Bring a medium saucepan of salted water to the boil. Blanch the sprouts for 2 minutes, then drain well. Heat the sunflower spread in a large frying pan over a high heat. When hot, add the sprouts, season well with salt and pepper and cook until the sprouts are golden.

Heat the remaining vegetable oil in a large frying pan over a moderately high heat. When hot, add half the kale leaves, season, and cook for a few minutes until crispy. Remove from the pan and drain on kitchen paper. Massage the remaining raw kale leaves between your fingers for 5 minutes.

To assemble, spread kale salsa on the bottom of four plates. Halve two of the butternut squash wedges, then place two full wedges, plus a half, on each plate. Top with the massaged kale and the crispy kale. Finish with the pickled butternut squash slices.

Beetroot and Pine Nut Tartlets

Sweet, nutty beetroots make such a vibrant and delicious start to any meal. This tart also makes a great lunch: just add a large green salad. The pine nut purée is something you can make in advance and store in the fridge as it works well with crackers or as a snack with fruit.

Serves 4

4 large red beetroots (about 300g)

2 tablespoons vegetable oil

sea salt and freshly milled black pepper

For the pastry

115g wholemeal flour, plus extra for dusting

50g non-dairy butter

½ teaspoon finely chopped rosemary leaves

½ teaspoon table salt

For the pine nut purée

100g pine nuts, toasted

4 tablespoons olive oil

2 tablespoons balsamic vinegar

½ candy (Chioggia) beetroot, peeled and finely sliced

½ yellow beetroot, peeled and finely sliced

Preheat the oven to 180°C/fan 160°C/gas mark 4.

Place the red beetroots on a sheet of foil, drizzle with the oil and season well. Wrap the foil around the beetroots and place in the oven for 1½ hours. Remove from the oven and unwrap the beetroots. When cool enough to handle, peel the beetroots, using a small knife. Slice each one into 8 wedges.

For the pastry, put the flour, butter, rosemary and salt in a food processor and pulse until the mixture resembles breadcrumbs. Add about 2 tablespoons of cold water to form a stiff dough. Shape into a ball, cover with clingfilm and refrigerate for 30 minutes.

Place the ball of pastry on a floured surface and roll out to 3mm thick. Transfer to a baking tray lined with parchment paper and return to the fridge for 20 minutes.

Preheat the oven to 190°C/fan 170°C/gas mark 5.

Put the pastry on its baking tray into the oven for 5 minutes. Remove and cut out 4 circles about 10cm in diameter. Return to the oven for a further 8–12 minutes until the pastry is golden and cooked through. Remove from the oven and put the pastry discs on a wire rack to cool.

Put three-quarters of the pine nuts in a blender with 25ml of water. Blend until smooth and creamy, seasoning with salt and adding a little more water if needed to form a smooth purée. Finely chop the remaining pine nuts.

To assemble, spread three-quarters of the pine nut purée over the pastry discs. Mix the olive oil and balsamic vinegar in a large bowl. Add the roasted beetroot wedges and the candy and yellow beetroot slices and season well with salt and black pepper, coating well in the dressing. Place a quarter of the beetroot slices, overlapping each other, on top of the pine nut purée. Pipe the remaining purée on top then garnish with the remaining slices and chopped pine nuts.

Cornbread, Refried Beans, Jalapeño Mole, and Smoky Blackberries

This is an ode to Mexican cuisine, without trying to replicate it, and uses flavours and textures I love, such as cornbread, refried beans and spicy jalapeños. The smoky blackberries add a slightly different dimension to the dish.

Serves 4

2 tablespoons non-dairy butter
4 x 2cm slices Cornbread (see page 166)
½ quantity of Jalapeño Mole
micro coriander cress, to garnish

For the refried beans

2 tablespoons non-dairy butter
1 onion, peeled and finely diced
1 garlic clove, peeled and finely grated
2 bay leaves
½ red chilli, deseeded and finely diced
½ teaspoon cumin seeds
½ teaspoon coriander seeds
200g canned pinto beans, drained and rinsed
sea salt and freshly milled black pepper

For the smoky blackberries

1 teaspoon lapsang souchong tea
25g caster sugar
2 tablespoons white wine vinegar
150g blackberries

Start with the refried beans. Heat the butter in a medium saucepan over a moderately high heat. Add the onion and season well with salt and black pepper. Cook until soft but not coloured. Add the garlic, bay leaves, chilli, cumin and coriander seeds and cook for a further 3 minutes. Add the beans with 200ml of water and simmer gently for 20 minutes until most of the liquid has evaporated. Remove the bay leaves and pulse-blend to a chunky paste. Keep warm.

For the blackberries, put 200ml of water in a small saucepan over a high heat and bring to the boil. Add the tea and sugar and allow to simmer for 2 minutes. Remove from the heat and allow to steep for 5 minutes. Strain through a fine sieve into a medium saucepan and add the vinegar. Set over a high heat and bring to the boil for 10 minutes. Pour over the blackberries and leave to macerate away from the heat.

Heat 1 tablespoon of butter in a non-stick frying pan over a high heat. Add 2 slices of the cornbread and brown on each side. Repeat with the remaining butter and cornbread.

To serve, place a piece of cornbread on each plate, top with the refried beans, then drizzle with the mole. Finish with the blackberries and garnish with the micro coriander cress.

Jalapeño Mole

zest and juice of ½ lemon
1 garlic clove, finely grated
2 jalapeños, from a can or jar (about 20g in total), roughly chopped
1 tablespoon rice wine vinegar
1 tablespoon jalapeño pickle juice from the can or jar
4 tablespoons finely chopped coriander
2 tablespoons finely chopped mint
60ml olive oil
1 teaspoon agave syrup
¼ teaspoon xanthan gum

Put all the ingredients in a blender and blitz until smooth. Scrape into a shallow container, cover with clingfilm and refrigerate. It will keep for 3 days.

Tempura Aubergine,
Black Sesame Sauce, Minted Guacamole

Aubergine has a wonderful unctuous texture. Encased in crispy tempura batter and silky in the centre, it really is hard to beat this vegetable when it comes to comfort food. Black sesame seeds have a slightly earthier flavour than white ones, but if you cannot find them use the white ones.

Serves 4

1 aubergine
table salt
vegetable oil, for frying
plain flour, for dusting
1 quantity of Tempura Batter (see page 180)
1 quantity of Black Sesame Sauce

For the minted guacamole

1 avocado, halved and stoned
8 mint leaves, finely chopped
8 coriander leaves, finely chopped
zest and juice of ½ lime
¼ teaspoon wasabi paste

Preheat the oven to 180°C/fan 160°C/gas mark 4.

Slice the aubergine into 8 wedges and cover the flesh liberally with table salt. Leave to sit for 20 minutes. Rinse off the salt and pat dry with kitchen paper. Set aside, uncovered, at room temperature until needed.

For the minted guacamole, scoop the avocado flesh into a mixing bowl. Mash with a fork, or using a stick blender. Add the remaining ingredients, season well and mix together or blend.

Fill a medium saucepan with vegetable oil to a depth of 5cm. Place over a moderate heat and heat to 190°C. Alternatively, heat the oil in a deep-fat fryer to 190°C.

Dust the aubergine wedges with flour, brushing off any excess using a pastry brush. Dip each wedge into the tempura batter, then gently lower into the hot oil. Fry just a few wedges at a time, so that the pan isn't too crowded. Fry for 3–4 minutes until golden. Remove with a slotted spoon onto kitchen paper and sprinkle with a little table salt. Repeat with the remaining ingredients.

To serve, place two aubergine wedges on each plate, then spoon the guacamole on the side. Drizzle with the black sesame sauce.

Black Sesame Sauce

70g black sesame seeds, toasted
1 tablespoon agave syrup
½ teaspoon table salt
2 tablespoons toasted sesame oil
1 tablespoon white miso paste

Put all the ingredients into a blender with 2 tablespoons of cold water and blend until smooth.

Salt-baked Carrots,
Pine Nut and Freekeh Crumb, Roast Garlic Aïoli

Salt baking is a wonderful way to cook any tubers or root vegetables. The seasoned dough encasing the vegetables creates a sealed cooking vessel which essentially steams the carrots while imparting them with seasoning from the salt and herbs.

Serves 4

4 large carrots, preferably a heritage variety

1 quantity of Salt Dough, made with rosemary

For the pine nut and freekeh crumb

100g wholegrain freekeh

2 tablespoons olive oil

2 tablespoons non-dairy butter

50g panko breadcrumbs

50g pine nuts, toasted and finely chopped

½ teaspoon finely chopped rosemary leaves

sea salt and freshly milled black pepper

½ quantity of Roast Garlic Aïoli (see page 184), to serve

Preheat the oven to 180°C/fan 160°C/gas mark 4. Line a baking sheet with parchment paper.

Wrap the carrots in the salt dough, place on the prepared baking sheet and transfer to the oven. Bake for 30–40 minutes until a knife goes through the dough and carrots with no resistance. Remove from the oven, chip off the salt dough and allow the carrots to cool slightly.

Cook the freekeh according to the packet instructions and strain off. Mix with the oil and season well.

To make the crumb, heat the butter in a large frying pan over a moderately high heat. Add the panko breadcrumbs and toast until golden. Add the cooked freekeh, pine nuts, rosemary and season with salt and black pepper. Mix well.

Scrape the carrots to remove any skin and the very salty layer. Cut each in half and garnish with the crumb. Serve with the aïoli.

Salt Dough

50g rock salt

100g flour

1 tablespoon chopped herbs

Mix the ingredients together in a large bowl. Add 65ml of cold water and mix together to form a stiff dough. Cover in clingfilm and refrigerate until needed.

French Onion Soup,
Roast Garlic Aïoli, Brioche Toastie

Rich and comforting, this is the perfect winter soup. I suggest making a large batch and keeping some in the freezer for a Sunday-night supper, when you need something to sustain you for the week ahead! The toasties make a delicious accompaniment. They can be made with any bread you wish if you do not have the time to make the brioche.

Serves 4

3 tablespoons non-dairy butter

4 onions, peeled and sliced

½ bunch of thyme, tied together with string

2 garlic cloves, peeled and finely sliced

200ml stout

3 litres Roasted Vegetable Stock (see page 180)

sea salt and freshly milled black pepper

1 quantity of Roast Garlic Aïoli (see page 184)

For the brioche toasties

80g non-dairy Cheddar-style cheese

40g non-dairy soft cheese

8 slices of Brioche (see page 167)

micro parsley, to garnish (optional)

Heat the butter in a large saucepan over a moderate heat. When melted, add the onions and thyme. Season lightly with salt and black pepper and cook for 15–20 minutes until golden. Add the garlic, cook for a further 5 minutes, then pour in the stout. Cook until the liquid has almost evaporated.

Add the stock to the pan and bring to a rapid simmer. Cook for 30–40 minutes until the liquid has reduced by half. Remove the thyme and adjust the seasoning if necessary.

For the toasties, preheat the grill to the hottest setting. Place the cheeses in a small saucepan over a low heat. Add a good grind of black pepper and stir the mixture until the Cheddar has melted and the cheeses have combined. Spread onto four of the brioche slices. Top with another slice of brioche and grill the toasties on both sides until golden.

Serve the hot soup with a good dollop of aïoli, parsley and the toasties on the side.

Caramelised Celeriac Soup,
Burnt Pear Purée, Hazelnut and Rosemary Pesto

Caramelising celeriac imparts it with a wonderful sweetness as well as
a slightly smoky taste. I continue that theme with a roasted pear purée,
offset by the nutty pesto.

Serves 4

2 pears
1 tablespoon olive oil
sea salt

For the soup
2 tablespoons non-dairy butter
1 celeriac, peeled and diced into
2cm chunks
2 bay leaves
1 teaspoon table salt
500ml non-dairy milk
2 litres Roasted Vegetable Stock (see
page 180)

For the pesto
1 tablespoon finely chopped
rosemary leaves
1 tablespoon finely chopped
flat-leaf parsley
30g toasted pine nuts
1 tablespoon nutritional yeast flakes
50g extra virgin olive oil

Preheat the oven to 180°C/fan 160°C/gas mark 4. Line a roasting tin
with foil.

Halve the pears, remove the core and place in the prepared roasting tin.
Bake for 1 hour. Remove from the oven, allow to cool a little and blend with
the olive oil and salt until smooth. Set aside.

For the soup, heat the sunflower spread in a large saucepan over a
moderate heat. When melted, add the celeriac, bay leaves and salt. Cook
until the celeriac is a deep golden colour, 15–20 minutes. Add the milk and
vegetable stock and simmer for 5 minutes. Blend until smooth and adjust
seasoning if necessary.

For the pesto, put all the ingredients in a blender and blend until a chunky
paste is formed. Season with salt and black pepper.

To serve, ladle the soup into bowls, top with a spoonful of pesto and a good
drizzle of pear purée.

Crispy Jerusalem Artichokes,
Nori, Lemon, Almond Purée

I always look forward to the time of year when Jerusalem artichokes come into season. They are great in soups and stews and take on a lovely sweetness when roasted. Nori is a very versatile ingredient to have to hand – use it as a garnish on salads or soups, or to add extra savouriness to any dish.

Serves 4

1.5kg Jerusalem artichokes, scrubbed
2 tablespoons vegetable oil
2 tablespoons non-dairy butter
¼ bunch of thyme
100g flaked almonds
2 tablespoons olive oil
sea salt and freshly ground black pepper
2 sheets of nori
12 slices of Confit Lemon (see page 39), to serve

Preheat the oven to 200°C/fan 180°C/gas mark 6.

Put the artichokes, vegetable oil, butter, thyme and seasoning in a roasting tray. Bake for 25–30 minutes, stirring every 10 minutes, until the artichokes are dark golden and the centres are soft.

Meanwhile, spread out the flaked almonds on a baking tray and roast in the oven for 10 minutes, stirring halfway through, until golden. Set aside 2 tablespoons of almonds. Put the rest in a blender jug with the olive oil and blend until a semi-smooth paste purée is formed. Season well with salt and black pepper.

Remove the artichokes from the oven, allow to cool slightly, then cut in half and put back on the roasting tray, adding a little more seasoning. Return to the oven for a further 5 minutes. Remove the thyme before serving.

Put the reserved toasted flaked almonds in a small blender jug with the nori and pulse to a crumb-like texture.

To assemble, share the artichokes between four plates. Arrange the confit lemon slices over the top, then drizzle with the almond purée. Sprinkle with the nori crumb and serve.

Braised Hispi Cabbage,
Dulse and Chestnuts

Braised cabbage takes on lovely sweetness. I am not the biggest seaweed fan, but, do really enjoy this dulse emulsion as it has a taste of the sea, as opposed to a fishy flavour. Fresh chestnuts are always one of winter's treats, so I try to make the most of them in salads and desserts.

Serves 4

1 hispi, or pointed, cabbage

2 tablespoons vegetable oil

1 teaspoon table salt

½ bunch of thyme

2 bay leaves

300ml Roasted Vegetable Stock (see page 180)

For the dulse butter

10g dried dulse

25ml olive oil

freshly milled black pepper

8 fresh raw chestnuts, peeled and finely sliced

½ nutmeg

Remove and discard the large, fibrous outer leaves from the cabbage. Cut the cabbage into 8 wedges. Heat the oil in a large saucepan over a high heat. When almost smoking, season the wedges with the salt and place in the hot oil. Brown on both sides – allow about 4 minutes each side. Add the thyme and bay leaves and cook for 2 minutes. Add 200ml of the stock, then cover the saucepan with a lid or foil and cook the cabbage for 5 minutes until a knife inserted meets with no resistance.

For the dulse butter, rehydrate the dulse according to the packet instructions. Place the oil in a small saucepan with 100ml of the vegetable stock. Bring to a simmer, then add the dulse. Cook for 3 minutes then blend to form a sauce. Season with black pepper and set aside.

To serve, place the cabbage wedges on a large serving platter. Drizzle with the cooking liquor, and dulse butter. Garnish with the chestnuts and finely grate the nutmeg over the top.

Winter Salad:
Roast Parsnip, Celeriac, Walnut Pesto, Pickled Apple, Crispy Rosemary

Sometimes a cold winter's day calls for something other than soup. This salad, while technically not a warming winter dish, will tick all the boxes when you are looking for a satisfying lunch. Swede often tends to get overlooked, but I find its crunchy texture rather delicious.

Serves 4

1 Granny Smith apple
100ml Mustard Pickle (see page 185)
vegetable oil, for shallow frying
2 sprigs of rosemary, leaves removed
2 parsnips, peeled
sea salt and freshly milled black pepper
½ celeriac, julienned
2 tablespoons coconut yogurt

For the walnut pesto
50g walnut halves
½ teaspoon thyme leaves
1 garlic clove, peeled
40ml walnut oil
1 teaspoon nutritional yeast flakes

Halve and core the apple, then slice into very thin semi-circles. Put the mustard pickle in a small saucepan and heat to a gentle simmer. Pour over the apple slices and set aside.

In a small saucepan, add enough vegetable oil to reach 2cm in depth. Place over a moderate heat until the temperature reaches 160°C. Fry the rosemary for 1 minute, in batches. Drain on kitchen paper and season with salt. Allow the oil to cool.

Preheat the oven to 180°C/fan 160°C/gas mark 4.

Cut the parsnips in half widthways, then into wedges. Toss in 2 tablespoons of the oil you used to fry the rosemary. Season well with salt and black pepper, spread out on a baking tray and bake for 20–25 minutes until golden.

Meanwhile, make the pesto. Spread out the walnuts on a baking tray and bake for 10 minutes. Remove from the oven and allow to cool.

Place the cooled walnut halves in a blender jug with the remaining pesto ingredients. Add 50ml of the rosemary oil, then pulse until a chunky pesto is formed. Season to taste.

Put the celeriac into a bowl and cover liberally with salt. After 5 minutes, add the coconut yogurt and season well with black pepper.

To assemble, place a good spoonful of pesto in the bottom of 4 bowls. Arrange the celeriac and parsnip on top. Garnish with the pickled apple and the crumbled crispy rosemary.

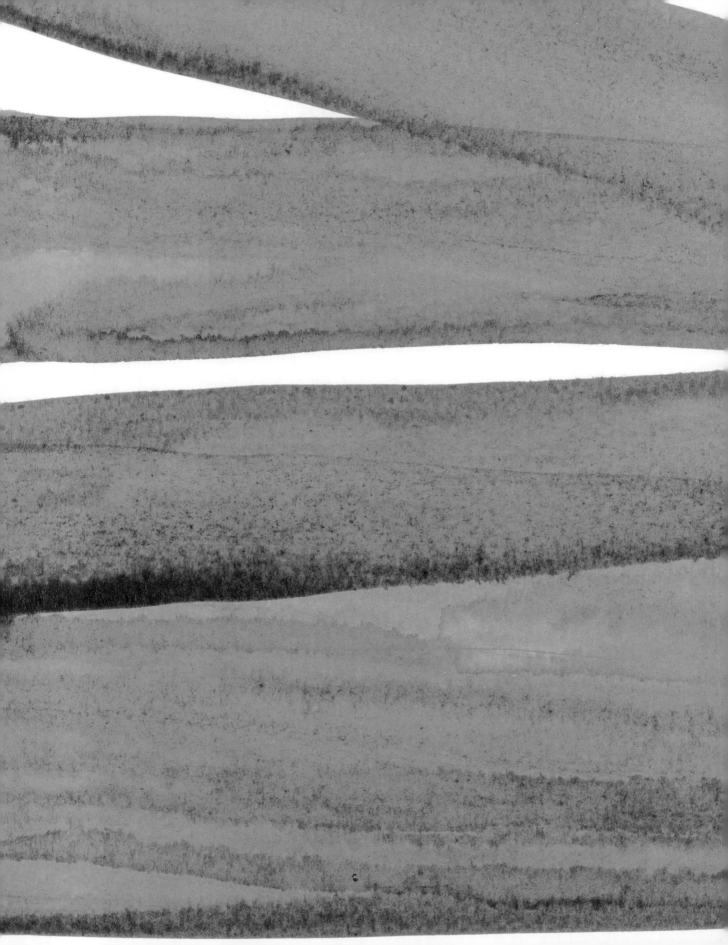

Mains

Swede Spaghetti,
Miso Emulsion, Parmesan and Brioche Crumbs

I had a dish that was very similar to this in New York in 2017. It was so delicious, and I felt swede was better than using pasta as it was less filling and the vegetable spaghetti added a sweet, slight crunchiness to the overall dish.

Serves 4

4 slices Brioche (see page 167)

2 tablespoons white miso paste
4 tablespoons extra virgin olive oil
100ml Light Vegetable Stock (see page 180)
sea salt and freshly milled black pepper

1 large swede, peeled and spiralised
½ bunch of flat-leaf parsley, leaves finely chopped
50g non-dairy Parmesan

Preheat the oven to 150°C/fan 130°C/gas mark 2.

Tear the brioche into small pieces and spread out on a roasting tray. Bake for 20 minutes until golden.

Put the miso paste and oil into a large saucepan over a medium heat. When heated, whisk together and add the vegetable stock. Season well with black pepper.

Bring a large pan of salted water to the boil. Plunge the swede into it and cook for 2–3 minutes until just al dente. Strain the swede, then add to the large saucepan containing the miso emulsion. Stir well, then add the parsley.

Share between 4 bowls, then grate the Parmesan over the top and crumble the brioche crumbs over.

Celeriac Gratin, Button Onions and Olive Sofritto

Sofritto is essentially a base sauce in many Latin cuisines. It always includes cooked onions, but the rest of the ingredients are wide ranging, depending on the origin of the cuisine. I have used red wine, tomatoes and olives in my version, which add a piquant complement to the gratin.

Serves 4

For the gratin

250ml oat cream

500ml non-dairy milk

4 sprigs of thyme

2 sprigs of rosemary

4 cloves

½ nutmeg, finely grated

2 bay leaves

50g non-dairy butter

1 tablespoon wholegrain mustard

1 large celeriac, peeled and cut into 5mm-thick slices

3 large floury potatoes, such as King Edward or Maris Piper, peeled and cut into 5mm-thick slices

sea salt and freshly milled black pepper

For the sofritto

2 tablespoons vegetable oil

1 onion, peeled and finely diced

1 leek, white part only, finely diced

1 celery stick, finely diced

2 garlic cloves, peeled and finely grated

1 tablespoon tomato purée

½ teaspoon smoked paprika

100ml red wine

100g stoned Kalamata olives, finely chopped

25ml olive oil

For the button onions

2 tablespoons non-dairy butter

200g pearl onions, peeled but left whole

1 tablespoon balsamic vinegar

Start by making the gratin. Put the cream, milk, thyme, rosemary, cloves, grated nutmeg and bay leaves into a large saucepan over a moderate heat. Bring to a gentle simmer for 15 minutes. Remove from the heat, cover and set aside for 15 minutes to allow the milk to infuse. Strain off the milk and whisk in the butter, mustard and seasoning.

Preheat the oven to 170°C/fan 150°C/gas mark 3.

Form a layer of overlapping celeriac slices in the base of an ovenproof gratin dish, about 20 x 20cm. Spoon over a little of the sauce, then repeat the process with a layer of potato slices. Continue until all the vegetables have been layered. Pour over any remaining sauce and finish with a good grinding of black pepper.

Place on a baking tray to catch any sauce that bubbles over and cook in the oven for 1–1½ hours until golden and a knife can be inserted with no resistance.

Start the sofritto 1 hour into the gratin cooking. Heat the vegetable oil in a large frying pan over a moderately high heat. When hot, add the onion, leek, celery and garlic and season well. Cook for 10 minutes or until soft. Stir in the tomato purée and paprika and mix well. Add the red wine and cook for 10 minutes until almost evaporated. Remove from the heat, add the olives and olive oil and mix well.

For the button onions, heat the butter in a medium frying pan until hot. Add the onions, season well and cook until brown all over. Add the vinegar and cook for a further 5 minutes until sticky.

Serve the gratin with the sofritto and onions on the side, with your favourite green vegetables.

Chicory and Mustard Cobbler

Cobblers can be both sweet and savoury and they are similar to a crumble, but instead of a crunchy topping they have scones on top. Chicory can be bitter, but takes on a lovely nuttiness when cooked and the natural sugars begin to caramelise.

Serves 4

25g non-dairy butter

3 red chicory, quartered lengthways

3 white chicory, quartered lengthways

100ml Roasted Vegetable Stock (see page 180)

sea salt and freshly milled black pepper

For the mustard sauce

75g non-dairy butter

75g plain flour

400ml non-dairy milk

250ml oat cream

½ bunch of thyme, leaves stripped

1 teaspoon Dijon mustard

2 tablespoons wholegrain mustard

1 teaspoon mushroom ketchup

For the scones

125g wholemeal flour

125g plain flour, plus extra for dusting

2 teaspoons baking powder

½ teaspoon mustard powder

2 tablespoons chopped flat-leaf parsley

½ teaspoon table salt

1 teaspoon freshly milled black pepper

75g non-dairy butter, frozen then grated

100g non-dairy Cheddar-style cheese, grated

100ml non-dairy milk, plus extra for glazing

2 tablespoons wholegrain mustard

First make the mustard sauce. Melt the butter in a medium saucepan. Add the flour, whisk well and cook for 30 seconds to 1 minute. Gradually whisk in the milk, cream and thyme and bring to a very gentle simmer. Cook for 15 minutes, whisking continuously, until thickened. Stir in the two types of mustard, mushroom ketchup and season with salt and black pepper. Cover the pan and keep warm, away from the heat.

For the scones, put the two types of flour, baking powder, mustard powder, parsley, salt and black pepper in a bowl and rub in the butter until the mixture resembles breadcrumbs. Mix in the cheese. Slowly add the milk and wholegrain mustard, mixing just to bring it all together into a firm dough; be careful not to overmix.

Roll out the dough on a floured surface to 5cm thick. Cover loosely with clingfilm and leave to rest for 10 minutes before cutting 8 circles using a 4cm cutter.

Preheat the oven to 180°C/fan 160°C/gas mark 4.

To cook the chicory, heat the butter in a large frying pan over a high heat. Place the red and white chicory quarters in the pan, cut-side down, and season well. Colour each side until deep golden, then pour in the stock and cook for a further 3 minutes. Transfer the chicory to a casserole dish and strain the cooking liquor into the mustard sauce, then whisk it in.

Pour the sauce over the chicory. Brush the scones with a little milk then place on top of the sauce, pressing them down gently to half-submerge in the sauce. Grind a good dose of black pepper over the top and a few pinches of sea salt.

Bake the cobbler for 20–25 minutes until the scones are cooked through and golden.

Slow-cooked Polenta,
Braised Mushrooms, Mushroom Gravy, Roasted Garlic and Thyme

Slow-cooked polenta doesn't need to involve constant stirring of a pot for hours. I learnt this technique when I spent a day in the kitchen at Dan Barber's Blue Hill at Stone Barns, in upstate New York. You cook it over a bain-marie, stirring fairly regularly, meaning it does not have the chance to stick to the bottom of the pan and also can cook at more of an even temperature.

Serves 4

For the polenta

1 litre Roasted Vegetable Stock (see page 180)

350g polenta (not quick cook)

50g non-dairy Cheddar-style cheese, grated

4 tablespoons extra virgin olive oil

sea salt and freshly milled black pepper

For the mushrooms

2 tablespoons non-dairy butter

1 onion, peeled and finely sliced

½ bunch of thyme, tied with kitchen twine

1 quantity of Mushroom Gravy (see page 116)

2 tablespoons vegetable oil

8 large, flat mushrooms, stalks removed

1 x quantity of Roasted Garlic Purée (see page 185), to serve

Preheat the oven to 180°C/fan 160°C/gas mark 4.

Have ready a saucepan that is one-third full of hot water.

Start by making the polenta. In another large saucepan, bring the vegetable stock to the boil. Transfer to a large bowl that will fit over the saucepan with the hot water. Whisk the polenta into the hot stock and season well with salt. Place the bowl over the saucepan. Set over a low heat and cover the bowl of polenta. After 20 minutes, whisk the polenta. Cover again and cook for a further 20 minutes. Whisk well, then add the cheese and oil, mixing well. Cover again and turn off the heat. Allow to sit, covered, for a further 10 minutes.

Meanwhile, for the mushrooms, put the butter into a large, deep frying pan over a moderately high heat. When hot, add the onion, seasoning well, along with the thyme. Cook for 10 minutes until golden. Add the gravy and cook for a further 5 minutes. Pour the sauce into a deep roasting dish.

Wipe out the frying pan, and heat 1 tablespoon of the vegetable oil until almost smoking. Season the mushrooms and add four of them to the pan. Brown well on each side, then add to the roasting dish. Repeat with the remaining oil and mushrooms.

Cover the roasting tray with foil and bake for 15 minutes. Remove the foil and the thyme, and bake for a further 5 minutes.

To serve, share the polenta between four bowls, then top with the mushrooms and gravy. Dollop over some roasted garlic purée and serve.

Roasted Parsnips,
Black Garlic, Port, Walnut Brown Rice

Black garlic is white garlic that has been very slowly caramelised at a low temperature over a period of anywhere from two to three months. It turns a wonderful black colour and has a very sweet, rich flavour, almost molasses-like. This process means it is not cheap, but a little goes a long way and in this dish it really lifts the overall result.

Serves 4

1kg parsnips, peeled and halved lengthways
2 tablespoons vegetable oil
½ bunch of rosemary
sea salt and freshly milled black pepper

250g brown basmati rice
80g walnuts, toasted and finely chopped
2 tablespoons walnut oil or olive oil
½ bunch of flat-leaf parsley, leaves picked and finely chopped

2 tablespoons non-dairy butter
1 onion, peeled and finely sliced
100ml ruby cooking port

2 black garlic cloves, frozen

Preheat the oven to 180°C/fan 160°C/gas mark 4.

Liberally brush the parsnips with the vegetable oil, then toss with rosemary, salt and black pepper. Spread out as a single layer in a roasting tray and roast for 10 minutes. Turn them over and roast for a further 10–15 minutes, depending on their thickness, until cooked through. Remove from the oven and set aside.

Cook the rice following the packet instructions and drain. Mix in the walnuts, walnut oil and parsley. Season well with salt and black pepper.

Heat the butter in a large frying pan. When hot, add the onion, seasoning well, and cook for 10–12 minutes until golden. Add the port and cook for a further 5 minutes until all the alcohol has evaporated.

To assemble, arrange the parsnips on a serving platter. Top with the rice, followed by the onion. Microplane the black garlic on top and serve.

Brussels Sprout, Chestnut and Sage Risotto

I am firmly in the camp of liking Brussels sprouts. When cooked right, they are nutty and moreish. They need to be cooked over a high heat, otherwise they will stew and go rather soggy. For contrasting textures, I like to use both cooked (vacuum-packed) as well as fresh chestnuts.

1.5 litres Light Vegetable Stock (see page 180)

2 bay leaves

½ bunch of sage, leaves picked and finely chopped, stalks reserved

270g cooked chestnuts, roughly chopped

200ml non-dairy milk

2 tablespoons vegetable oil

1 onion, peeled and finely diced

1 garlic clove, peeled and finely grated

500g carnaroli or Vialone Nano risotto rice

125ml dry white wine

75g non-dairy Parmesan, grated, plus extra for garnish

2 tablespoons non-dairy butter

300g Brussels sprouts, halved

4 sprigs of thyme, leaves picked

8 fresh chestnuts, peeled and finely sliced

sea salt and freshly milled black pepper

Put the stock in a large saucepan with the bay leaves and sage stalks and bring to the boil. Reduce the heat and gently simmer.

Put 180g of the cooked chestnuts into a saucepan with the milk. Season well and bring to a simmer for 5 minutes. Remove from the heat and blend to make a smooth chestnut purée. Set aside.

Heat the oil in a large saucepan over a medium heat. Add the onion and garlic, and season well. Cook for a few minutes until the onion has softened but not coloured.

Add the rice and stir for a few minutes until the grains become shiny and translucent. Add the wine and cook until the alcohol has evaporated.

Add a ladleful of the hot stock and continue stirring until the stock has been absorbed by the rice. Add the remaining stock, a ladleful at a time, stirring continuously until each ladleful has been absorbed before adding the next – this should take 15–20 minutes. Set aside 100ml of hot stock. The risotto is cooked when the rice grains are a little firm but don't have any chalky crunch on the outside when bitten into.

Add the chestnut purée and Parmesan to the risotto and mix well. Turn off the heat and cover the pan while you cook the sprouts.

For the sprouts, Heat the butter in a medium frying pan until very hot. Add the sprouts, cut-side down, and thyme. Season well and cook until a deep golden brown. Turn each sprout over and add the reserved hot stock to the pan. Cook for a further 3 minutes, then remove from heat.

To finish the risotto, add the remaining chopped, cooked chestnuts to the risotto with the chopped sage. Spoon onto warm plates and top with the sprouts, fresh chestnuts and parmesan.

Roasted Jerusalem Artichokes,
Puy Lentils, Zhoug and Spiced Prune

Lentils are a great store cupboard ingredient to have all year round to use in salads, soups and also as a garnish for a dish. Puy lentils, from Le Puy in France, are a type of green lentil and have a shorter cooking time than other green lentils. Their earthy flavour marries well with the sweetness of roasted artichokes. Micro herbs are simply small herb shoots. They have an intense flavour and also add colour and texture to dishes, without having to use whole leaves.

Serves 4

1.5kg Jerusalem artichokes, scrubbed
¼ bunch of thyme
50g non-dairy butter
250ml non-dairy milk
sea salt and freshly milled black pepper

280g dried Puy lentils, or green lentils
2 bay leaves
1 garlic clove
¼ bunch of thyme
2 tablespoons olive oil
¼ bunch of flat-leaf parsley, leaves finely chopped

80g pitted prunes, roughly chopped
½ teaspoon ground cinnamon
½ nutmeg, finely grated
½ teaspoon ground mixed spice

1 quantity of Zhoug (see page 181), to serve

To garnish (optional)
micro purple sorrel
micro parsley

Preheat the oven to 180°C/fan 160°C/gas mark 4.

Put the artichokes in a roasting tray with the thyme and butter and season with salt. Roast for 20–25 minutes, moving the artichokes around every 10 minutes, until they are uniformly a deep golden colour and crispy.

Remove from the oven and blend half the artichokes with the milk to form a thick purée. Season to taste and set aside in a warm place.

Meanwhile rinse the lentils well under cold water. Put in a pan with 1 litre of water, the bay leaves, garlic and thyme. Season well, then bring to the boil. Simmer for 20–30 minutes for Puy lentils, and 30–40 minutes for green lentils, until cooked through. Drain, discarding the herbs and garlic, then mix through the oil, salt and black pepper and parsley.

Put the prunes in a medium saucepan with the spices and cover with 100ml hot water. Bring to a simmer for 10 minutes, then lightly pulse in a blender, or use a stick blender, to create a chunky paste. Season well with salt.

To serve, share the purée between four bowls. Add the lentils and prunes, then top with the artichokes, with some halved. Drizzle with the zhoug and garnish with the micro sorrel and micro parsley.

Swiss Chard and Chickpea Pancakes,
Turmeric and Coconut Sauce

Chickpea, or gram, flour is another good ingredient to have in your store cupboard. It creates a richer texture and flavour than plain wheat flour and is a source of protein. This turmeric and coconut sauce is versatile and can be used as a base for curries and soups, or as a sauce to have with rice or pasta.

For the turmeric and coconut sauce

2 tablespoons vegetable oil

2 shallots, peeled and sliced

3cm knob of ginger, peeled and sliced

5cm knob turmeric, bashed

20g cashew nuts, toasted

½ teaspoon table salt

400ml coconut milk

For the pancakes

4 tablespoons vegetable oil

½ teaspoon cumin seeds

1 onion, peeled and finely diced

1 garlic clove, peeled and finely grated

500g Swiss chard, finely chopped

125g chickpea flour

1 teaspoon baking powder

150ml non-dairy milk

sea salt and freshly milled black pepper

For the chickpea salsa

100g canned chickpeas, roughly chopped (drained weight)

½ bunch of coriander, leaves finely chopped and stalks reserved

½ green chilli, finely diced

1 tablespoon sesame oil

zest and juice of 1 lime

For the turmeric and coconut sauce, heat the oil in a large saucepan. When hot, add all the ingredients, apart from the coconut milk. Season well. Cook for 10 minutes until lightly coloured then add the coconut milk. Simmer for 20 minutes, then blitz in a blender until smooth. Set aside in a warm place.

To make the pancakes, heat half the oil in a large saucepan over a moderate heat. When hot, add the cumin seeds and cook for 2 minutes. Add the onion and garlic and cook until soft. Add the chard and cook through for 4–5 minutes until wilted. Remove from the heat.

Put the chickpea flour, baking powder and seasoning in a large bowl. Add the milk and mix until just combined. Add the cooled chard and mix to combine.

Heat ½ tablespoon of the remaining oil in a small frying pan. Ladle a quarter of the pancake mix into the hot butter. Cook for a few minutes until golden, gently flip over and cook on the other side until cooked through. Remove from the pan and set aside in a warm place. Repeat with the remaining mix.

For the chickpea salsa, mix all the ingredients together and season well.

Serve the pancakes drizzled with the spicy sauce and the salsa on the side.

Turnip Fondants,
Turnip Marmalade, Baby Turnip and Fennel Salad

Turnips, like sprouts, are another unsung hero and this recipe uses them three ways. New season spring turnips have a much lighter flavour than those that have been stored in the cooler months. Vegetable marmalade is also something you can make with many vegetables; it works well with fennel and also carrots. The natural sugars in the vegetables caramelise and become very sweet.

Serves 4

6 turnips
50g non-dairy butter
2 bay leaves
¼ bunch of thyme
250ml Roasted Vegetable Stock (see page 180)
sea salt and freshly milled black pepper

For the turnip and fennel salad
1 bunch of baby turnips, halved
½ fennel bulb, finely sliced
½ quantity of Basic Vinaigrette (see page 186)
¼ bunch of tarragon, leaves finely chopped
½ teaspoon fennel seeds, toasted and lightly crushed

4 slices of rye bread
2 tablespoons olive oil

Peel the turnips and slice each one in half lengthways. Using a ring cutter, cut out the centre of each slice. Grate the trimmings.

Heat half the butter in a medium saucepan over a moderate heat. Add the grated turnip, season well with salt and cook slowly, stirring regularly, for 1 hour, until you have a golden marmalade.

Meanwhile, for the turnip fondants, melt the remaining butter in a frying pan large enough to fit the 12 slices of turnip. Spread it evenly around the pan and season well. Put the turnips into the butter and season again. Arrange the herbs, then pour the stock on top and place the pan over a moderate to high heat. Cover the turnips with a circle of parchment paper and leave to cook for 20 minutes. Turn the turnips over and cook for a further 10 minutes. Remove the turnips from the pan and keep warm. Increase the heat and rapidly simmer the liquid until a syrupy consistency is reached.

Preheat the grill.

For the salad, mix all the ingredients together and season well.

Tear the rye bread into chunks. Toss in the oil and season well, then spread out onto a baking tray and gently grill until warm and lightly toasted.

To assemble, place 3 fondants on each plate. Drizzle with the reduced sauce. Divide the turnip marmalade between the plates and serve with the salad and croûtons.

Spring Pea and Broad Bean Gnudi,
Asparagus, Confit Lemon and Fennel

Gnudi are traditional little Italian ricotta dumplings. The name, which means 'nude', applies because they are akin to a filled ravioli, minus the pasta. The gnudi can be made the night before and stored in the fridge, covered by the semolina, then boiled the next day. The semolina forms a shell on the outside of the gnudi so they hold their shape when cooked. You can use frozen peas and broad beans in this recipe too, if that is what is available.

Serves 4

450g peas (50g retained and the other 400g blanched and refreshed)

200g broad beans, blanched, refreshed and popped out of their skins

½ nutmeg, finely grated

zest of 1 lemon

250g Soya Ricotta (see page 183)

125g non-dairy Parmesan, finely grated, plus extra to serve

120g semolina

½ teaspoon table salt

50ml extra virgin olive oil

juice of 1 lemon

½ bunch of tarragon, leaves chopped

1 bunch (8–12 spears) of asparagus

½ fennel bulb

50g Confit Lemon (see page 39), finely chopped

sea salt and freshly milled black pepper

Put the blanched peas, broad beans, nutmeg, lemon zest, salt and black pepper into a blender and pulse to a chunky paste. Scrape the mixture into a large mixing bowl and add the ricotta, Parmesan and half the semolina. Mix to form a wet dough. Put the remaining semolina in a deep dish. Roll the dough into 20 small balls and drop them into the semolina as each one is rolled. Shake the dish to coat the gnudi and refrigerate for at least 1 hour.

Mix the olive oil, lemon juice and tarragon together in a large bowl. Season well. Snap the woody ends off the asparagus then, using a vegetable peeler, shave the spears into thin strips. Finely slice the fennel, using a mandoline if you have one, and add, along with the asparagus, to the bowl with the olive oil dressing.

When ready to serve, bring a large pan of salted water to the boil. Carefully lower the gnudi into the water, in batches, and cook for 3–4 minutes until they float to the top. Remove with a slotted spoon and drain on kitchen paper.

Put 5 gnudi on 4 plates. Season the salad then dress the plates with the reserved raw peas, fennel, asparagus and lemon confit. Grate a little Parmesan over the top and serve.

Salt-baked Sweet Potato,
Mint and Coconut Emulsion, Crispy Quinoa

This is one of those dishes that ticks all the boxes for me. It is sweet, a little spicy, salty and has a great crunch added to it with the quinoa. Try using the yellow-fleshed sweet potato – I grew up on them in New Zealand where we call them kumara. The flesh is slightly drier than the orange-fleshed ones and the flavour more honey-like.

Serves 4

1 quantity of Salt Dough (see page 63)

4 sweet potatoes, scrubbed clean

250g cooked quinoa (left overnight in the fridge to dry it out)

2 tablespoons desiccated coconut

1 teaspoon onion seeds

1 tablespoon vegetable oil

sea salt and freshly milled black pepper

For the mint and coconut emulsion

1 bunch of mint, leaves picked and stalks discarded

100ml coconut cream

1 green chilli, roughly chopped

1 garlic clove, peeled and finely grated

¼ bunch of coriander

zest and juice of 1 lime

2 tablespoons rice wine vinegar

½ apple, peeled and cored

Preheat the oven to 180°C/fan 160°C/gas mark 4.

Roll out the salt dough and wrap each sweet potato in the dough. Place on a baking tray in the oven for 1 hour until a skewer inserted into the centre meets no resistance. Remove from the oven and allow to sit for 10 minutes before breaking open the salt dough.

Mix the quinoa with the coconut, onion seeds, oil and a good amount of salt and black pepper. Spread out onto 2 baking trays and bake for 8 minutes. Stir well then return to the oven for a further 8 minutes until golden and crispy.

For the mint and coconut emulsion, put all the ingredients in a blender and blend until smooth. Season well with salt.

To serve, slice the sweet potatoes into 1cm-thick slices. Drizzle the emulsion over the top and garnish with the crispy quinoa.

Jersey Royals,
Pickled Dulse, Samphire Pesto, Wild Rice and Smoked Sea Salt

Jersey Royals are another wonderful springtime ingredient. Heralding from Jersey and grown right next to the sea, these new potatoes have a subtle saltiness to them, as well as a hint of seaweed. Out of season, other new potatoes will work very well too. The pickled dulse will be more flavoursome if you make it a day in advance.

Serves 4

600g Jersey Royal potatoes, scrubbed
250g mixed wild rice
1 teaspoon smoked sea salt

For the pickled dulse
10g dried dulse
50ml rice wine vinegar
2cm knob of ginger, peeled and finely grated
1 tablespoon grated palm sugar
25ml toasted sesame oil

For the samphire pesto
100g samphire
25g non-dairy Parmesan
30g flaked almonds
50ml olive oil

Begin by pickling the dulse. Rehydrate the dulse according to the packet instructions. Mix the other ingredients together. Drain the dulse and finely chop. Pour the pickling liquor over the dulse and set aside.

For the samphire pesto, put all the ingredients in a blender and pulse until a chunky pesto is formed. Season to taste.

Put the potatoes in a large saucepan of salted water and bring to the boil. Cook for 15–20 minutes until tender. Drain well, then gently break in half and mix through the pesto.

While the potatoes are cooking, cook the wild rice according to the packet instructions. Drain well. Gently mix through the pickled dulse, including the liquor.

Put the rice on a large platter and top with the potatoes. Season with the smoked salt and serve.

Crispy Globe Artichokes,
Spelt and Tarragon Stuffing, Salsa Verde

Preparing globe artichokes can be a little time consuming, but it is well worth it. Use gloves to avoid stained hands. Instead of the larger ones, you can get the smaller Violet artichokes, which are delicious. Look for upright and bright artichokes as they begin to droop as they get old.

Serves 4

1 lemon, halved
6 globe artichokes
2 tablespoons vegetable oil
2 tablespoons non-dairy butter
sea salt and freshly milled black pepper

For the stuffing

160g spelt
2 slices of bread, broken into chunks
zest of 1 lemon
60g Brazil nuts, toasted
½ bunch of tarragon
2 tablespoons non-dairy butter
1 onion, peeled and finely diced
1 garlic clove, peeled and finely grated

1 quantity of Salsa Verde
parsley, to garnish

Preheat the oven to 180°C/fan 160°C/gas mark 4.

Fill a deep bowl with 2 litres of cold water and squeeze the lemon juice into the water. To prepare the artichokes, cut one-third off the tip of each artichoke. Snap off the outer petals until you start to see pale yellow petals. Trim the top again from the artichoke so you expose the furry 'choke'. Scoop out the furry part, using a spoon, and discard. Using a peeler, peel the hard outer layer from the stem, until you reach the pale flesh. Place each prepared artichoke into the lemon water to prevent them browning.

Heat the oil in a large frying pan. When almost smoking, add the artichokes, season with salt and brown off, in batches, until golden, then place in a roasting tray. Melt the butter and drizzle over the artichokes. Season well with salt and black pepper and roast for 15 minutes, then remove from the oven to cool slightly.

Meanwhile, make the stuffing. Cook the spelt according to the packet instructions, then drain. Put the

bread, lemon zest, Brazil nuts and tarragon into a blender and pulse to a crumb-like consistency. Heat the butter in a frying pan and when hot, add the onion and garlic, season well with salt, and cook until soft. Mix the spelt with the breadcrumbs and onions and season well with salt and black pepper.

Stuff the artichokes with the stuffing and return to the oven for 10 minutes.

Serve with salsa verde and a green salad.

Salsa Verde

2 tablespoons chopped tarragon leaves
2 tablespoons chopped flat-leaf parsley
2 tablespoons capers
zest and juice of 1 lemon
100ml extra virgin olive oil
salt, to season

Put all the ingredients in a blender and pulse until a chunky paste is formed.

Grilled Asparagus,
Homemade Ricotta and Toasted Hazelnut Tortellini, Yuzu Emulsion

The combinations in this recipe work so well together. Yuzu juice is now readily available in supermarkets, which is great as it is one of my favourite flavours. Used commonly in Japanese cooking for flavouring and seasoning, it is more subtle than lemon juice and has a far less aromatic scent and flavour.

Serves 4

For the tortellini

100g blanched hazelnuts, toasted
¼ bunch of tarragon, leaves only
zest of 1 lemon
1 quantity of Soya Ricotta (see page 183)
20 gyoza wrappers
sea salt and freshly milled black pepper

For the yuzu emulsion

25ml yuzu juice
50ml extra virgin olive oil
½ teaspoon agave syrup

2 bunches (16–24 spears) of asparagus
2 tablespoons olive oil
sea salt and freshly milled black pepper

To garnish (optional)

edible flowers
micro parsley

Begin by making the tortellini. Put the hazelnuts, tarragon, lemon zest and some seasoning in a blender and pulse until crumbs are formed. Add to the ricotta and mix well. To assemble the tortellini, place a gyoza wrapper on your worktop and brush the outer centimetre of it with water. Put a teaspoonful of the filling in the top half of the wrapper, leaving a border of at least 1cm. Fold the wrapper in half and press the edges together with your thumb and forefinger, excluding any air. With your thumb, make an indentation in the centre of the filling. Let the border of the wrapper curl upwards as you bring the two pointed edges together. Secure the two points by pinching with a little water. Repeat with the remaining wrappers and filling. Set the tortellini aside until ready to serve.

For the emulsion, whisk the yuzu juice, oil and agave syrup together, then set aside.

Snap off the woody ends of each asparagus stalk and trim the ends to neaten them. Heat a griddle pan and bring a large saucepan of salted water to the boil. Blanch the asparagus, in batches if you don't have a large enough saucepan, draining well on kitchen paper. Drizzle with the oil, season well, then place on the hot griddle until charred.

Steam the tortellini for 5 minutes until cooked through. They can also be boiled in water, but you need to be careful they do not burst.

Share the asparagus between 4 plates, adding 5 tortellini to each, then drizzle with the yuzu dressing and garnish with the edible flowers and micro parsley, if using.

Purple Sprouting Broccoli,
Black Sesame Pappardelle, Garlic and Pumpernickel Crunch

Purple sprouting broccoli has more bite and is a little more earthy than normal green broccoli. When preparing, do not trim off the leaves – they're delicious! The black sesame pappardelle adds a nuttiness to the dish making it a very satisfying main course.

Serves 4

1 quantity of Black Sesame Pasta (see page 182)

plain flour, for dusting

2 tablespoons olive oil

2 large slices pumpernickel bread, broken into chunky crumbs

500g purple sprouting broccoli

sea salt

For the dressing

50ml toasted sesame oil

1 tablespoon rice wine vinegar

2 tablespoons Roasted Garlic Purée (see page 185)

2 tablespoons black sesame seeds, toasted

¼ bunch of flat-leaf parsley, leaves finely chopped

Divide the pasta dough into 3. Using a little flour, roll out each piece into a rectangle about 5mm thick. If you have a pasta machine, roll the dough through a few times, reducing the thickness setting each time until you reach a thickness of 2mm. If you do not have a pasta machine, roll the dough by hand to a thickness of 2mm. Once you have rolled all three pieces, cut the rectangles into 1cm wide long strips. Cover with a tea towel and leave to rest.

For the dressing, whisk all the ingredients together and season to taste.

Heat the oil in a large frying pan. When hot, add the pumpernickel crumbs, seasoning well. Cook until golden.

Bring 2 large pans of salted water to the boil. Drop the pasta into one and cook for 3–4 minutes until al dente, then drain. Blanch the broccoli in the other pan for 4–5 minutes until tender. Drain the broccoli and mix with the dressing.

Arrange the pappardelle in 4 bowls and top with the broccoli and pumpernickel crumbs.

Spinach, Leek and Oregano Kataifi Pie

Kataifi pastry is finely shredded filo dough used to make Greek, Turkish and Middle Eastern pastries. It adds a lot of texture to a dish and can be used for both sweet and savoury recipes. It's a great thing to keep handy in the freezer.

Serves 4

500g baby or large leaf spinach
100g non-dairy butter
2 onions, peeled and finely diced
1 garlic clove, peeled and finely grated
1 whole nutmeg, finely grated
2 leeks, white part only, cut into 2cm rounds
400g kataifi pastry, defrosted if frozen
200g Hummus
1 bunch oregano, leaves picked
1 tablespoon black onion seeds
sea salt and freshly milled black pepper

Preheat the oven to 190°C/fan 170°C/gas mark 5.

Bring a large saucepan of salted water to the boil. Blanch the spinach, in three batches, for 30 seconds, and refresh in iced water. Drain in a colander, then take small handfuls and squeeze out all the excess water. Roughly chop the spinach.

Heat 25g of the butter in a large saucepan over a moderate heat. When hot, add the onions and garlic, seasoning well. Cook for 5–7 minutes until the onions are soft, but not coloured. Add the spinach and the nutmeg and mix well. Season to taste.

Heat another 25g of the butter in a large frying pan over a high heat. When hot, add the leeks, season and colour well on each side.

Melt the remaining butter and spoon 25g into a 23cm tart ring set on a baking sheet. Press half the kataifi pastry into the bottom of the ring. Spread the hummus over the top, then top with the leeks. Finish with the spinach, pressing down to create an even layer. Scatter over the oregano then top with the remaining kataifi dough. Brush with the remaining melted butter and season with salt and black pepper. Garnish with the onion seeds.

Bake for 20–25 minutes until golden and cooked through.

Hummus

240g canned chickpeas, drained and rinsed
60g tahini
1 garlic clove
zest and juice of ½ lemon
25ml olive oil
½ teaspoon agave syrup
½ teaspoon table salt
freshly milled black pepper

Put all the ingredients in a blender or food processor. Blend to a smooth paste, adding 20–30ml water until the desired consistency is achieved.

Courgette and Cumin Fritters,
Miso, Grilled Courgette and Cashews

These fritters make a satisfying and tasty meal. You can also substitute the courgettes for aubergines, or use a combination of both. The fritter mix can be made up to two days in advance and stored in the fridge until needed. It is a good recipe to use up any courgettes that are coming to the end of their best.

Serves 4

For the fritters

1kg courgettes, grated

1 tablespoon table salt

100g spelt

3 tablespoons vegetable oil

1 onion, peeled and finely diced

1 garlic clove, peeled and finely grated

2 teaspoons cumin seeds, toasted and crushed

4 tablespoons wholewheat or spelt flour

zest of ½ lemon

4 tablespoons chopped flat-leaf parsley

1 green chilli, deseeded and finely diced

80g non-dairy Cheddar-style cheese, grated

sea salt and freshly milled black pepper

2 yellow or green courgettes, cut into 5mm-thick ribbons

1 tablespoon olive oil

80g cashew nuts, roasted and roughly chopped

1 quantity of Miso Vinaigrette

Put the grated courgettes in a colander and sprinkle with the salt. Set over a bowl and leave for 30 minutes to drain.

Cook the spelt according to the packet instructions. Drain well.

Heat 1 tablespoon of the vegetable oil in a frying pan over a moderate heat. When hot, add the onion and garlic and cook, without colouring, until soft. Add the cumin, mix well, then transfer to a mixing bowl.

Put the courgettes in a clean tea towel and squeeze out as much of the liquid as possible. Tip into the mixing bowl with the onion and garlic. Add the flour and lemon zest and mix well. Stir in the parsley, chilli, cheese, spelt and a good grinding of black pepper. Divide the mix into 4 and shape into patties. Refrigerate until needed.

Heat a griddle pan until almost smoking. Drizzle the courgette ribbons with the olive oil and season well with salt and black pepper. Grill each side until nicely charred and cooked through.

To cook the fritters, heat the remaining 2 tablespoons of vegetable oil in a large, non-stick frying pan over a high heat. Fry the patties, in batches, for 3–4 minutes on each side, until golden on the outside and cooked through.

To serve, place a fritter on each plate, top with the cashew nuts and courgette ribbons. Drizzle with the miso vinaigrette and serve.

Miso Vinaigrette

1 tablespoon white miso paste

2 tablespoons rice wine vinegar

80ml olive oil

1 tablespoon toasted sesame seed oil

Whisk the miso paste with the rice wine vinegar and 25ml of cold water, until smooth. Add the oils and whisk together. Always whisk or shake before use to ensure the mix has emulsified properly.

Chargrilled Runner Beans,
Romesco, Tofu, Oregano and Lemon Panzanella

Runner beans work really well chargrilled and don't take long to cook either.
They partner comfortingly with the sweet, peppery Romesco sauce and
my homemade tofu, which has a texture – and flavour – that is completely
different from most tofu you can buy, so do try making your own. It doesn't
take long and the setting agents have a long shelf life.

Serves 4

For the panzanella

zest and juice of 2 lemons

100ml tomato juice

splash of Tabasco sauce

½ teaspoon celery salt

25ml olive oil

4 slices of sourdough bread

600g runner beans, topped

2 tablespoons vegetable oil

sea salt and freshly milled black pepper

1 quantity of Tofu (see page 181)

1 quantity of Romesco Sauce (see page 36)

½ bunch of oregano, leaves picked

Mix the lemon zest and juice, tomato juice, Tabasco, celery salt and olive oil
together. Tear the bread into bite-sized chunks and pour over the dressing.

Heat a griddle pan or barbecue until hot. Toss the beans in the vegetable
oil and season well. Grill until charred on the outside and almost cooked
through in the centre. Remove the beans from the pan and chargrill the
bread on both sides.

To serve, pile the beans on a serving platter and spoon over the tofu.
Top with the panzanella, dollop on the Romesco sauce and finish with
oregano.

Radish and Mooli
with Ricotta and Herb Salad

We are spoiled by the number of different varieties of radishes now readily available. People mostly enjoy them raw for their crunch, but they develop a lovely nutty flavour when cooked – and lose some of their heat too. When pickled, the colour from the skin dyes the flesh, so they take on a delicate pink hue and a tangy crunch.

Serves 4

½ mooli

½ quantity of Mustard Pickle (see page 185)

1 watermelon (or red meat) radish

2 bunches of breakfast or heritage radishes, stems on

50ml rice wine vinegar

zest and juice of 1 lime

2 tablespoons agave syrup

¼ bunch of basil, leaves picked

¼ bunch of dill, leaves picked

¼ bunch of mint, leaves picked

2 tablespoons vegetable oil

sea salt and freshly milled black pepper

1 quantity of Soya Ricotta (see page 183)

Peel and slice the mooli into 3mm-thick slices, using a mandoline if you have one. Put the mustard pickle in a small saucepan and bring to the boil. Pour over the mooli and refrigerate for at least 2 hours.

Peel and slice the watermelon radish into 2mm-thick slices.

Halve the breakfast or heritage radishes, keeping the stems on one of the halves, separating into two piles: one with stems, one without.

Mix the rice wine vinegar, lime zest and juice and agave syrup together. Add the herbs and set aside.

Heat the oil in a large frying pan. When hot, season the radishes without the stems with salt, and add to the pan, cut-side down. Cook until nicely golden, then remove from the pan.

Put the breakfast radishes with the stems in a bowl. Add the herb dressing, season well and gently mix.

To serve, divide the ricotta between 4 plates. Top with a mixture of radishes and drizzle with the remaining dressing.

Chargrilled Spring Onions,
Watercress Sauce, Spaetzle, Summer Mushrooms

Spaetzle are small German dumplings that are similar in texture to pasta. They are very simple to make and you use a colander to form the small droplets, dropped straight into boiling water. They can be made in advance, chilled in cold water and strained, and refrigerated, to use when needed. For the watercress sauce, do take the time to remove the leaves from the stems, as this will ensure a bright green sauce, as opposed to a dull brown one.

Serves 4

For the watercress sauce

50g non-dairy butter

1 small baking potato, such as King Edward, peeled and very thinly sliced

½ teaspoon table salt

½ teaspoon coarse ground black pepper

500ml Light Vegetable Stock (see page 180)

1 bunch of watercress, leaves picked and chopped, stalks finely chopped

100g spinach leaves, finely chopped

¼ teaspoon English mustard

For the spaetzle

100g plain flour

¼ teaspoon mustard powder

50g aquafaba

1 teaspoon wholegrain mustard

30ml non-dairy milk

25g non-dairy butter

250g seasonal mushrooms

2 tablespoons Madeira

sea salt and freshly milled black pepper

12 spring onions

Before you start, prepare everything you need to blend the watercress sauce quickly: blender, fine sieve, ladle and a large bowl in an ice bath.

Heat the butter in a large pan. When melted, add the potato and cook until soft. Stir in the salt, black pepper and half the stock. Add the watercress stalks and bring to the boil. Cook until the stalks are soft; it should take 1–2 minutes. Stir in the remaining stock, bring to the boil and add the watercress and spinach leaves. Cover the pan with a lid and cook for 3 minutes. Remove from the heat and blend quickly, with the mustard, to a smooth green sauce. Pass through a sieve into the bowl on ice. Whisk in the bowl so it cools quickly and maintains its vibrant green colour. Taste and add a little more salt if necessary. Cover and refrigerate.

For the spaetzle, put the flour, mustard powder and seasoning in a bowl. Whisk the aquafaba and mustard together in a separate bowl, then mix into the flour. Add the milk and beat until smooth. Bring a large saucepan of salted water to the boil. Pour the batter through a colander into the boiling water. When the spaetzle rise to the top, scoop out and refresh in iced water.

To cook the mushrooms, heat the butter in a frying pan over a high heat. When bubbling, add the mushrooms, seasoning well. Cook until most of the liquid has evaporated. Add the Madeira and cook for a further 4 minutes. Add the drained spaetzle and cook until hot.

For the spring onions, heat a chargrill pan to as hot as possible. Brush them with the oil, season well, then grill until charred and al dente.

To serve, share the mushrooms and spaetzle between four plates. Top with the spring onions, drizzle with the sauce and garnish with watercress sprigs.

Barbecued Baby Gem,
Sweetcorn Pudding, Barbecued Onions and Kimchi

Barbecued lettuce is a really delicious way to do something different
with lettuce other than using it in salad. If you don't have a barbecue, a
griddle pan will work just as well, but do ensure it is as hot as can be.

Serves 4

For the sweetcorn pudding

4 corn on the cobs

1 onion, peeled and halved

2 bay leaves

½ bunch of tarragon, leaves picked and
chopped, stalks retained

¼ bunch of thyme

50g non-dairy butter

100ml coconut milk

50g non-dairy Cheddar cheese, grated

1 teaspoon onion seeds

sea salt and freshly milled black pepper

For the onion wedges

1 teaspoon onion seeds

25g plain flour

½ teaspoon mustard powder

2 garlic cloves, peeled and finely grated

½ teaspoon smoked paprika

2 red onions, peeled and cut into
6 wedges each

2 tablespoons vegetable oil

4 baby gem lettuces

2 tablespoons vegetable oil

100g Kimchi (see page 29),
finely chopped

Preheat the oven to 180°C/fan 160°C/gas mark 4.

Start with the sweetcorn pudding. Cut the kernels off the sweetcorn by
standing the cobs on their end and cutting downwards. Put the trimmed
cobs in a large saucepan and cover with water. Add the onion, bay leaves,
tarragon stalks and thyme to the pan. Set over a high heat and bring to the
boil for 30 minutes. Strain off the liquid into another saucepan. Bring to the
boil and allow to reduce until you have 400ml of liquid remaining.

Put the butter in a large frying pan over a moderately high heat and add
the corn kernels, seasoning well with salt and black pepper. Cook through,
then remove half the kernels. Add the reduced corn stock and coconut milk
to the frying pan and simmer for 5 minutes. Blend until smooth then add
to the reserved sweetcorn kernels, with the tarragon leaves. Transfer to an
ovenproof casserole and top with the grated cheese, onion seeds and black
pepper. Bake for 15 minutes until golden and heated through.

For the onion wedges, mix together the onion seeds, flour, mustard powder,
garlic and smoked paprika. Add a good amount of salt and black pepper.
Coat the onion wedges in the mix and drizzle with the oil. Heat a griddle pan
or barbecue until hot, then grill the onions on all sides for 12–15 minutes
until golden and cooked through.

Cut the baby gem lettuces in half lengthways. Drizzle with the oil, season
well, then grill for 6–8 minutes until golden on the outside and almost
cooked through.

To serve, place the onions and baby gem on a platter, drizzle with the kimchi
and serve alongside the sweetcorn pudding.

Whole Barbecued Spiced Cauliflower,
Tarragon Tzatziki, Summer Slaw

Barbecued Cauliflower is not normally thought of, but give it a try as it is absolutely delicious. Brining it ensures it is seasoned all the way through. The spice mix does not have too much heat in it, so up the chilli flakes if you prefer. Using the cauliflower leaves in the slaw also minimises waste.

Serves 4

For the cauliflower brine

7g table salt

2 bay leaves

1 teaspoon coriander seeds

1 large cauliflower, leaves removed and reserved for the slaw

For the spice mix

25g non-dairy butter

1 tablespoon soft brown sugar

½ teaspoon table salt

1 teaspoon cumin seeds, toasted

1 teaspoon yellow mustard seeds

½ teaspoon chilli flakes

1 teaspoon coriander seeds

½ teaspoon mustard powder

1 teaspoon smoked paprika

For the tzatziki

½ cucumber, grated

½ teaspoon cumin seeds, toasted

125g coconut yogurt

¼ bunch of mint, leaves chopped

¼ bunch of tarragon, leaves chopped

sea salt and freshly milled black pepper

For the summer slaw

¼ red cabbage, finely sliced

1 nectarine, halved, stoned and julienned

100g sugar snap peas, finely sliced

100g rocket, finely chopped

2 tablespoons sesame seeds, toasted

¼ bunch of coriander, leaves finely chopped

50ml Sesame Vinaigrette (see page 186)

First make the cauliflower brine. Bring 100ml of water to the boil with the salt, bay leaves and coriander seeds. When the salt has dissolved, add 900ml of cold water and submerge the cauliflower in it for 2 hours.

Preheat a barbecue or griddle pan until hot. Combine all the spice mix ingredients, then remove the cauliflower from the brine, pat dry, and brush all over with half the spiced butter. Place on the hot barbecue or griddle pan. Cook all over until a deep golden, then brush with the remaining spiced butter and wrap in foil and put back on the barbecue or pan. Cook in the foil for 20–25 minutes until a skewer inserted into the centre meets no resistance. Remove the cauliflower from the foil and place back on the barbecue, drizzling the cooking juices from the foil over the top.

For the tzatziki, mix all the ingredients together and season to taste.

For the summer slaw, mix all the ingredients together, including the sliced cauliflower leaves, then season well and dress with the vinaigrette.

Slice the spiced cauliflower and serve drizzled with the tzatziki and the slaw on the side.

Borlotti Beans,
Fermented Tomato, Basil and Chickpeas

Fermentation is something that has become a lot more popular in everyday cooking in recent years. The health benefits of it are very sound and it is a really simple thing to do. It does take a little planning in advance though in order to get the maximum flavour. I suggest starting the tomatoes for this recipe 4 days ahead. You should start to see a few bubbles around the tomatoes, but this is normal as it is the bacteria doing its thing. I have specified San Marzano tomatoes as I find their sweet richness is unbeatable, but any seaonal, ripe tomato will work well.

Serves 4

For the fermented tomatoes

1 teaspoon table salt

50ml rice wine vinegar

50ml balsamic vinegar

1 teaspoon agave syrup

1 tablespoon tomato purée

6 San Marzano tomatoes

250g podded borlotti beans

1 carrot, peeled and cut into 4

1 celery stick, top removed, cut into 4

1 bay leaf

¼ bunch of thyme

1 teaspoon smoked paprika

100g non-dairy cream cheese

2 tablespoons tomato purée

1 bunch of basil, leaves picked and stalks retained

200g cooked chickpeas, roughly chopped

½ quantity of Hummus (see page 99)

2 tablespoon olive oil

extra virgin olive oil, to garnish

Start by fermenting the tomatoes. Mix all ingredients together, apart from the tomatoes, and add the basil stalks. Add 100ml of cold water. Prick the tomatoes all over with a skewer, then place in a container or jar and cover with the liquid. Loosely cover and leave in a slightly warm, dark place for a minimum of 4 days.

Place the beans, carrot, celery, bay leaf and thyme into a medium saucepan. Top with water, then place on a high heat. Bring to the boil and simmer gently for 25–40 minutes until soft (note the cooking time will vary depending on how fresh the beans are). Strain off the liquid from the pan, removing the carrot, celery and herbs.

Place the smoked paprika, cream cheese and tomato purée into a bowl. Whisk well. Place in a pan with the cooked borlotti beans and heat through.

To assemble, chop the basil leaves, reserving a few for garnish, and mix with the chickpeas, hummus and olive oil, seasoning well. Place the hummus around the edge of the serving plate, then place the beans on top. Peel the skin from the tomatoes (it will come off very easily after the fermentation) and slice each in half. Arrange on top, drizzling over a little of the fermenting liquor. Garnish with the reserved basil leaves and olive oil, then serve.

Slow-cooked Aubergines,
Tamarind, Roasted Onion, White Bean Purée

Cannellini beans are such a handy store cupboard ingredient. These white beans can be used for salads, soups, curries and also blended to make a wonderfully creamy purée. If you have not used tamarind before it has a rich, slightly sour taste.

Serves 4

2 aubergines

2 tablespoons olive oil

2 tablespoons vegetable oil

2 onions, peeled and halved from root to tip

2 tablespoons non-dairy butter

300ml Roasted Vegetable Stock (see page 180)

sea salt and freshly milled black pepper

For the white bean purée

150ml non-dairy milk

2 bay leaves

2 tablespoons non-dairy butter

400g can cannellini beans, drained and rinsed

For the tamarind sauce

50g tamarind paste

100ml Roasted Vegetable Stock (see page 180)

1 tablespoon agave syrup

1 tablespoon cornflour

coriander, to garnish

Preheat the oven to 180°C/fan 160°C/gas mark 4.

Halve the aubergines lengthways and score the flesh with diagonal lines. Drizzle with the olive oil and season well with salt. Place in a roasting tray, cover with foil and roast for 30 minutes. Remove the foil and roast for a further 20 minutes.

Meanwhile, set an ovenproof saucepan or frying pan over a moderate heat and add the vegetable oil. When hot, put the onions, cut-side down, into the oil. Season well with salt and brown for 8 minutes until golden, then add the butter and cook for a further 8 minutes. Pour over the stock, bring to the boil, then cover with the pan with a lid or foil. Transfer to the oven and roast for 30 minutes. Once cooked, remove the onions from the pan and reserve the liquid.

For the bean purée, put the milk, bay leaves and butter in a saucepan. Bring to a gentle simmer then remove from the heat, add the beans and cover and set aside to infuse for 20 minutes. Remove the bay leaves, then blend the beans until smooth, adding more milk if needed. Season well and keep warm.

For the tamarind sauce, put the tamarind paste, stock and agave syrup in a medium saucepan. Add the cooking liquor from the onions, bring to a simmer and season well. Mix the cornflour with 1 tablespoon of water, then whisk into the sauce. Remove from the heat and pour through a fine sieve.

To serve, place a large dollop of white bean purée onto each plate and add an aubergine half. Using a fork, peel apart the layers of each onion and add to the plates. Finish with the tamarind sauce.

Braised and Crispy Broccoli,
Mushroom Gravy, Toasted Barley

The stalk of broccoli has a lovely crunch – in fact, it's my favourite part – so it never ends up in the compost bin. Just peel back the tough outer skin before using. It's also delicious raw and finely sliced.

Serves 4

2 tablespoons olive oil

150g pearl barley

1 onion, peeled and finely diced

1 garlic clove, peeled and finely grated

sea salt and freshly milled black pepper

2 heads of broccoli

2 bay leaves

¼ bunch of thyme

2 garlic cloves, peeled

1 tablespoon soy sauce

2 tablespoons vegetable oil

1 quantity of Mushroom Gravy, to serve

Heat the olive oil in a medium saucepan. When hot, add the barley, onion, garlic and seasoning and fry for 5 minutes until toasted. Add 200ml water, mix well and allow to simmer until the water has been absorbed. Keep adding a little water and stirring frequently until the barley is al dente, about 20 minutes.

While the barley is cooking, make the mushroom gravy.

Remove the broccoli florets, keeping the stalks intact and removing the hard outer layer. Put the bay, thyme, garlic and soy sauce in a large saucepan and half fill with water. Season with salt and black pepper and bring to the boil. Add the florets and cook for 2 minutes. Strain, return the water to the saucepan and bring back to the boil. Add the stalks, ensuring they're covered by water. Cook for 5 minutes, then remove and slice in half.

Heat the vegetable oil in a large frying pan. Fry off the broccoli florets, in batches, until crispy, seasoning well.

To serve, pile the barley on a large platter. Add the stalks and florets and pour over the mushroom gravy.

Mushroom Gravy

1 tablespoon vegetable oil

2 onions, peeled and halved

2 garlic cloves, peeled

30g dried porcini mushrooms

600g flat mushrooms, finely sliced

½ bunch of thyme

2 bay leaves

1 teaspoon Marmite

1 teaspoon tomato paste

6 black peppercorns

1 tablespoon cornflour

sea salt and freshly milled black pepper

Heat the oil in a large saucepan over a high heat. When hot, add the onions and colour until well browned. Add the garlic and brown for a further 2 minutes. Add 4 litres of water and the remaining ingredients except the cornflour and seasoning. Reduce to a low simmer for 2 hours. Strain off the liquid into another saucepan, discarding the vegetables. Simmer the liquid for 20–30 minutes until about 1 litre of stock remains.

Mix the cornflour with 2 tablespoons of water and whisk into the stock. Cook for 3–4 minutes until thickened. Adjust the seasoning to taste.

Spelt Tagliatelle,
Crispy Rosemary, Kabocha Squash and Hazelnut Butter

It is hard to beat a comforting bowl of pasta. Frying rosemary gives it a crispy texture that adds a nice crunch to any dish. Kabocha squash are small, green-skinned pumpkins that have a dry, sweet flesh. They have a low moisture content, which works very well when roasted.

Serves 4

1 kabocha squash, peeled, deseeded and sliced into 2cm wedges

100ml vegetable oil, for shallow frying, plus 2 tablespoons

1 bunch of rosemary

1 quantity of Spelt Pasta (see page 182)

1 quantity of Hazelnut Butter (see page 184)

sea salt and freshly milled black pepper

Preheat the oven to 180°C/fan 160°C/gas mark 4.

Put the squash in a roasting tray and coat with 2 tablespoons of oil. Season liberally with salt and black pepper, then roast for 20–25 minutes until golden.

Heat the vegetable oil in a medium saucepan over a moderately high heat. When the temperature reaches around 120°C fry the rosemary sprigs, in batches, for 1 minute. Drain on kitchen paper and season well with salt. When cooled, pull the leaves off the stalk.

Roll out the pasta and put through a pasta machine to a thickness of 2mm, then through the tagliatelle cutter. If you do not have a pasta machine, dust your worktop with a little spelt flour and roll out the pasta, in four batches, to a thickness of 2mm, then cut into strips. Bring a large pan of salted water to the boil, add the tagliatelle and cook for 3–5 minutes until al dente. Drain off.

Stir three-quarters of the hazelnut butter through the pasta. Add the squash and rosemary and gently mix. Share between 4 bowls, then top with the remaining hazelnut butter and serve.

Sage and Shallot Tart,
Kale and Cobnut

Sage is such an aromatic and savoury herb it instantly gives further depth of flavour to a dish. I generally associate it with the colder months of the year, and this tart uses cobnuts, which are in season in autumn. If you cannot source them use hazelnuts instead – they're very similar.

Serves 4

1.2kg banana shallots, peeled and halved lengthways

3 tablespoons vegetable oil

½ bunch of thyme

2 tablespoons balsamic vinegar

200ml non-dairy milk

2 tablespoons non-dairy butter

200ml Roasted Vegetable Stock (see page 180)

sea salt and freshly milled black pepper

200g mixed kale

½ quantity of Puff Pastry (see page 182) or 1 sheet (320g) ready-rolled vegan puff pastry

1 teaspoon non-dairy butter, melted

½ bunch of sage

100g fresh cobnuts, peeled and roughly chopped

Finely slice 400g of the halved shallots. Heat 1 tablespoon of the oil in a large saucepan and, when hot, add the sliced shallots and thyme and season well. Cook over a medium heat until the shallots begin to caramelise. When they are a deep golden colour, which will take about 20 minutes, add the balsamic vinegar and mix well. Cook for a further 4 minutes until sticky. Add the milk and remove the thyme stalks. Blend using a stick blender to form a smooth purée. Cover the pan with clingfilm and set aside.

Heat two large frying pans over a high heat with 1 tablespoon of oil in each. When hot, put the shallot halves in the pans, cut-side down, and season well with salt. Cook for 6–8 minutes until the shallots are deeply caramelised. Divide the butter between the pans and cook for a further 4 minutes. Add 100ml of the stock to each pan, then cover with a lid or foil and allow the shallots to cook for 10 minutes until soft.

Bring a large saucepan of salted water to the boil and blanch the kale, in batches, for 1 minute. Strain off and plunge into iced water. When cool, strain off and squeeze out any excess moisture.

Preheat the oven to 200°C/fan 180°C/gas mark 6.

Place the pastry sheet on a greased baking tray. Gently score a 1.5cm border around the edges of the pastry and make indentations in it with a fork.

Put the shallot purée in the centre of the tart and smooth out, leaving the border of the pastry clear. Top the purée with the kale. Arrange the cooked shallot halves over the tart, along with the sage leaves.

Bake for 16–20 minutes, until the pastry is golden. Garnish the tart with the sliced cobnuts and serve.

Crispy Chickpea Cakes,
Roasted Butternut Squash, Harissa and Pumpkin Seed Mole, Pickled Celery

These chickpea cakes are delicious. I pondered over what to call them as they are not cakes as such, but they are slightly gooey and incredibly moreish, so they are like cake in that respect. Mole originates from Mexico and generally means a thick, spicy sauce. This one is almost like a pesto.

Serves 4

1 butternut squash
1 sprig of rosemary
2 tablespoons olive oil
1 tablespoon non-dairy butter
sea salt and freshly milled black pepper

For the pickled celery

2 stalks celery
¼ quantity of Mustard Pickle (see page 185)

For the mole

1 tablespoon harissa paste
100g pumpkin seeds, toasted
1 tablespoon tahini
2 tablespoons olive oil
1 tablespoon coriander, finely chopped
½ teaspoon cumin seeds, toasted

½ quantity of Chickpea Chips (see page 180), to serve
plain flour, for dusting
lemon balm, to garnish

Begin by pickling the celery. Finely slice the celery. Gently warm the mustard pickle in a saucepan, then pour over the celery. Refrigerate for at least 2 hours.

Preheat the oven to 180°C/fan 160°C/gas mark 4.

Peel the butternut squash, halve lengthways and remove the seeds using a spoon. Put the skin and seeds into a medium pan with the rosemary, and cover with water. Place over a medium heat and simmer for 1 hour, then strain, discarding the skin, seeds and rosemary and reserving the stock. Set aside.

Meanwhile, dice the squash flesh into 2cm cubes. Toss in the oil, season well with salt and black pepper, then spread out on a roasting tray. Roast for 15–20 minutes until golden.

Reserve half the squash that is most in tact. Put the remaining squash into a saucepan, cover with the stock and simmer for 10 minutes. Strain, reserving the liquid. Combine with the butter in a blender, add a little of the cooking liquid and blitz until smooth. Add more liquid if necessary, to form a thick purée. Season to taste and set aside to keep warm.

For the mole, put all the ingredients in the blender and blitz until a smooth sauce is formed.

To serve, portion the chickpea chips into 8 pieces. Dust with flour and gently pan fry in oil. Serve with the warm purée, roasted squash, mole, pickled celery and lemon balm.

Cavalo Nero and Split Pea Biryani

I am a big fan of biryani; it is the perfect comfort food with a delicious spice infusion. I have taken inspiration for this recipe from a wonderful cook, and friend, Sabrina Ghayour. I enjoyed the crispy base of her version so much, which is called a tahdig in Persian cuisine. When I was making her recipe for the first time she advised to make loads of the crispy onions; it was sound advice!

Serves 4

150ml vegetable oil, plus an extra 25ml

4 onions, peeled and finely sliced

180g yellow split peas, rinsed well

400ml coconut milk

400g basmati rice, washed until the water runs clear

pinch of saffron threads

25g non-dairy butter

250g cavalo nero

sea salt

For the spice base

3 garlic cloves, peeled and finely grated

4cm knob of ginger, peeled and finely grated

4cm knob of turmeric, peeled and finely grated

1 green chilli, finely diced

2 bay leaves

12 cardamom pods

2 cinnamon sticks

1 tablespoon cumin seeds

To serve

coconut yogurt

1 bunch of coriander, leaves finely chopped

Heat 150ml of vegetable oil in a large frying pan over a moderately high heat. When almost smoking, add the onions and salt and cook for 20–25 minutes, until golden and crispy. Remove with a slotted spoon onto kitchen paper to drain. Retain the oil.

Pour half the retained oil into a large saucepan and set over a medium heat. When hot, add all the ingredients from the spice base. Season with a little salt and cook for 5 minutes until fragrant. Add 300ml of warm water and the split peas, stirring well. Cover with a lid and simmer gently for 25 minutes, stirring regularly. Add the coconut milk and simmer for a further 5 minutes.

While the spice base is cooking, bring a large saucepan of salted water to the boil. Add the rice and part-cook for 6 minutes. Drain well.

Put the saffron in a small bowl and pour over 50ml of boiling water.

Line the base of a medium to large saucepan with a circle of parchment paper. Put 25ml vegetable oil, plus the butter, on top of the paper and set over a moderately high heat. When hot, layer a third of the rice on the base. Spoon over a little of the saffron water. Layer half the split pea mix on top, followed by half the cavalo nero leaves and a third of the crispy onions. Repeat the layers. Top with the remaining third of rice, the saffron water and onions. Cover with a firmly fitting lid and cook over a low–medium heat for 40 minutes. Don't be tempted to lift the lid and check while cooking, as the steam will escape, which is needed to cook the rice.

Check the biryani after 40 minutes to see if the rice is al dente. If so, it is ready. If not, leave for a further 10 minutes.

When ready serve with coconut yogurt and coriander alongside.

Roasted Cauliflower,
Caramelised Purée, Pickled Stems, Deep Fried Leaves, Capers and Lemon

Cauliflower takes on a nutty taste when cooked for longer than 20 minutes. If you cook it for less, it does run the risk of being a little soapy in flavour. This recipe uses the whole cauliflower, including the leaves, meaning there is very little waste. The leaves are also delicious when deep fried.

Serves 4

2 cauliflowers

¼ quantity of Mustard Pickle (see page 185)

6 tablespoons vegetable oil

50ml non-dairy milk

2 tablespoons capers

8 cornichons, finely chopped

1 tablespoon chopped flat-leaf parsley

1 tablespoon olive oil

table salt and freshly milled black pepper

2 teaspoons Baked Citrus Jam (see page 44), to serve

Remove the leaves from the cauliflower and cut the stems from the centre, reserving both. Halve the stems if they are really large. Gently heat the mustard pickle, then pour over the stems and set aside.

Cut both the cauliflowers into four slices and separate out the two large centre slices from both. Set aside. Chop the remaining smaller slices into small pieces.

Heat 2 tablespoons of the oil in a medium saucepan over a moderately high heat. Add the chopped cauliflower, season well and cover with a lid. Cook for 5 minutes, stir, then cook for a further 5 minutes with the lid on. Remove the lid and cook for a further 10–15 minutes until the cauliflower is a deep golden colour. Add the milk, then blend to form a smooth purée.

Heat two large frying pans over a high heat with 1 tablespoon of vegetable oil in each. When hot, add two slices of cauliflower per pan and fry to a dark gold colour. Flip the slices over and repeat on the other side. When both sides are coloured, cover both pans with foil, or a lid, and turn down the heat to medium. Cook for a further 10 minutes until soft.

Mix the capers, cornichons, parsley and olive oil together. Season with black pepper.

Heat the remaining vegetable oil in a frying pan over a moderate heat. When hot, fry the cauliflower leaves until they turn a dark brown then remove with a slotted spoon onto kitchen paper, season and set aside.

To assemble, heat the purée and share between four plates. Place a slice of cauliflower on top then add the caper dressing. Dollop the Citrus Jam on top, then finish with the pickled stems and crispy leaves.

Desserts

Orange, Polenta and Olive Oil Cake,
Licorice, Burnt Orange

This cake is delicious on its own. It has a wonderful moist texture that is enhanced by the polenta. The licorice adds another dimension, and if you are not keen on the flavour please try it anyway – I have experienced a lot of people who enjoy the licorice cream, but are not licorice fans. I may be slightly biased, but the soft licorice from New Zealand has the best flavour and texture!

Serves 8

1 orange
25ml orange liqueur
35g caster sugar
½ teaspoon table salt

For the orange, polenta and olive oil cake

200g ground almonds
50g yellow quick-cook polenta
80g plain flour
1½ teaspoons baking powder
100g aquafaba
200g caster sugar
100g olive oil
1 orange, quartered, pips removed
100g non-dairy butter, melted
icing sugar, for dusting

For the cream

2 x 32g soft licorice sticks, roughly chopped
150g non-dairy cream cheese

Preheat the oven to 170°C/fan 150°C/gas mark 3. Grease and line a 20cm square cake tin.

Put the orange into a baking dish and place in the oven for 1½ hours, or until a deep golden brown.

For the cake, put the almonds, polenta, flour and baking powder in a bowl and mix together. Whisk the aquafaba in a stand mixer until stiff peaks form. Gradually add the sugar and whisk until the sugar has dissolved.

Put the oil and orange into a blender and blitz to a smooth paste. Add the melted butter and blitz again, then add this mixture to the dry ingredients. Fold in gently to just combine. Fold in the meringue then pour the mixture into the prepared cake tin. Bake for 30–40 minutes until a skewer inserted into the centre comes out clean. Place the tin in the fridge immediately, to prevent the cake from sinking.

For the cream, put the licorice into a medium saucepan and cover with warm water. Set over a medium heat and simmer for about 20 minutes, until the licorice is soft, topping up with more water if necessary. Pour the entire contents of the pan into a blender and blitz until a smooth paste forms. You may need to add a little more water. Put the soft cheese in a bowl and whisk until smooth. Whisk in the licorice, then cover and refrigerate.

Put the cooked orange into the blender with the orange liqueur, caster sugar and 100ml of warm water. Blend until a smooth paste is formed. Add the salt and pass through a fine sieve to remove any lumps.

To serve, dust the cake with icing sugar, then slice into 8 pieces. Serve with a small spoonful of the burnt orange purée and spoon the licorice cream onto the plate.

Dark Chocolate Fondant,
Salted Caramel Coconut Ice Cream

Oozy chocolate fondants have to be one of life's most simple pleasures. Always use good-quality chocolate. High percentage of cocoa solids give a richer flavour – experiment with different chocolate for the centre and the fondant. I love a rich centre so usually go for a 72%.

For the fondants

100g dark chocolate, minimum 70% cocoa solids, broken into pieces

75g Cashew Butter (see page 184)

75g aquafaba

50g caster sugar

¼ teaspoon xanthan gum

40g rice flour

½ teaspoon baking powder

80g ground almonds

For the fondant centre

50g dark chocolate, minimum 70% cocoa solids, broken into pieces

20g coconut oil

For the salted caramel coconut ice cream

195g caster sugar

500ml coconut milk

100g non-dairy milk

½ teaspoon xanthan gum

1 teaspoon table salt

1 teaspoon cocoa powder, for dusting

Begin by making the fondant centres. Melt the chocolate and coconut oil in a bowl over a saucepan of simmering water. Whisk in 40ml of water, then pour into six mini muffin moulds, or small (3cm) moulds. Freeze for at least 4 hours.

For the ice cream, put the sugar in a medium, heavy-based saucepan over a moderately high heat. Gently shake the pan when you see the sugar start to melt. Do not stir or you may cause the caramel to crystallise. As the sugar keeps melting, keep shaking and swirling the pan until a deep caramel is formed. Put the coconut milk and non-dairy milk in a saucepan and bring to a simmer. When a deep caramel is reached, carefully pour in the milk mixture and xanthan gum, whisking well. Add the salt and continue to whisk to allow the caramel and milk to fully mix. Pour through a fine sieve and place in the fridge to cool. Once cool, churn in an ice-cream maker following the manufacturer's instructions, or transfer to the freezer and remove and whisk every hour to break up the ice crystals.

For the fondants, grease 4 ramekins, 150–200ml each. Melt the chocolate and cashew butter in a bowl over a saucepan of simmering water. Keep warm. Whisk the aquafaba to stiff peaks, using a stand mixer or hand-held mixer. Gradually add the sugar, whisking until glossy and no sugar remains. Add the xanthan gum and whisk for a further 3 minutes.

Combine the rice flour, baking powder and ground almonds, then mix into the melted chocolate. Fold in the meringue and mix until just combined.

Spoon one-eighth of the fondant mix into each ramekin then place a fondant centre in the middle of each one. Top with the remaining fondant mix. Transfer to the freezer and freeze for a minimum of 2 hours.

Preheat the oven to 170°C/fan 150°C/gas mark 3.

Bake the fondants for 7 minutes from frozen. Remove from the oven, dust with the cocoa powder and serve.

Peanut Butter Pudding,
Peanut Caramel, Dark Chocolate Sorbet

This is one of those desserts that ticks all the boxes for a luscious treat – peanut butter, caramel and chocolate. You can make the puddings as well as the sorbet in advance and freeze until needed. The sorbet is also delicious on its own – it makes a little more than you need for 4 people.

Serves 4

For the peanut butter pudding

80g aquafaba

80g caster sugar

65g ground almonds

65g plain flour

½ teaspoon baking powder

pinch of salt

20g peanut butter

20g olive oil

20g non-dairy butter, melted

20ml non-dairy milk

For the dark chocolate sorbet

125g caster sugar

90g cocoa powder

90g dark chocolate, minimum 70% cocoa solids, broken into pieces

100g ice

For the peanut butter caramel

60g caster sugar

30g non-dairy butter

60ml non-dairy milk

1 tablespoon peanut butter

¼ teaspoon table salt

Preheat the oven to 180°C/fan 160°C/gas mark 4. Grease 4 ramekins, approximately 250ml in volume.

Start by making the sorbet. Put the sugar and cocoa powder in a saucepan with 200ml of water. Whisk well, then place over a medium heat and bring to the boil. Continue whisking and cooking the mixture until it thickens, about 5 minutes. Put the chocolate in a mixing bowl and pour the cocoa mix through a fine sieve onto the chocolate. Allow to sit for 5 minutes, then whisk together. Add the ice and whisk until the ice has melted and the mixture has cooled. Churn in an ice-cream maker following the manufacturer's instructions, or transfer to the freezer and remove and whisk every hour to break up the ice crystals.

For the puddings, whisk the aquafaba in a stand mixer until stiff peaks form. Gradually add the sugar and whisk until glossy and all sugar grains have dissolved.

In a separate bowl, combine the ground almonds, flour, baking powder and salt. In a third bowl, mix the peanut butter, olive oil, melted butter and milk together. Stir the peanut butter mix into the dry ingredients, then gently fold in the meringue. Divide between the ramekins and bake for 10 minutes.

When ready to serve, make the caramel. Put the sugar into a small, heavy-based saucepan or frying pan. Set over medium heat and leave the sugar to melt, swirling the pan occasionally for even caramelisation. Once the sugar has dissolved and reached a deep golden colour, add the butter and whisk to combine well. Bring the milk to the boil, then add to the caramel and whisk well. Lastly, whisk in the peanut butter and salt.

Drizzle the warm caramel sauce over the peanut puddings and serve with a big scoop of dark chocolate sorbet.

Blackberry and Sloe Gin Trifle

Trifle was always a firm favourite on our Christmas day dining table. My Nana used to make it with tinned pineapple and lashings of cream sherry. Here, I have used seasonal blackberries, with lemon curd and sloe gin. The earthy flavour of the gin enhances the autumnal feel and is an alternative to sherry. The topping is made in a cream whipper – a metal canister powered by gas that whips cream – which were popular in the 1970s. They are a useful piece of kitchen equipment, but if you don't have one you can serve pouring cream on the side.

Serves 8

For the sponge
100g aquafaba
100g caster sugar
100g plain flour
1 teaspoon baking powder
25g ground almonds
40g non-dairy butter, melted
zest of ½ lemon

For the jelly
50g blackberry jam
½ 6.5g sachet Vege-Gel (vegan gelatine)
100ml sloe gin

For the custard
300ml non-dairy cream
250ml coconut milk
3 tablespoons custard powder
60g caster sugar

For the cream topping
120ml oat cream
120ml coconut milk
60g coconut yogurt
½ teaspoon xanthan gum
1 teaspoon vodka
½ teaspoon agave syrup

250g blackberries, halved
½ quantity Lemon Curd (see page 184)
Edible flowers, to garnish

Preheat the oven to 170°C/150°C fan/gas mark 3. Grease an 18cm cake tin.

For the sponge, whisk the aquafaba in a bowl with an electric whisk, or using a stand mixer, until stiff. While still whisking, gradually add the caster sugar. Whisk until stiff and glossy. Place the flour, baking powder and ground almonds in a bowl and mix well. Fold in the meringue, then gently mix through the melted butter and lemon zest. Pour the batter into the prepared cake tin and bake for 18–20 minutes, until a skewer inserted in the centre comes out clean. Allow to cool in the tin for 20 minutes, then remove and cool completely on a wire rack.

For the jelly, place the jam into a saucepan with 250ml of water and the Vege Gel. Bring to the boil, then whisk for 3 minutes. Add the gin, pour into a medium size dish and place in the fridge to set.

For the custard, place all ingredients in a medium size saucepan. Bring to a gentle simmer, stirring constantly, until the custard thickens. Pour into a container, cover with clingfilm directly touching the surface of the custard, and refrigerate until cold.

For the cream topping, whisk everything together and place into a cream gun. Charge with one cartridge of gas and refrigerate until needed.

To assemble, cut the sponge and jelly into 1cm pieces. Combine with the blackberries, and place in the bottom of a trifle bowl. Dot small spoonfuls of the lemon curd on top of the sponge and blackberry mix. Whisk the custard, then spread on top. Top with the cream just prior to serving, and sprinkle with the edible flowers.

Quince Clafoutis with Yogurt Sorbet

A clafoutis is a French dessert, a little like a Dutch pancake. It can be made with all stone fruit, including peaches, cherries and apricots. I like to make mine with a caramel on the base, which adds a little richness to the finished product. Quinces always signify the beginning of autumn for me, and I love how their pale yellow flesh turns such a blush pink colour when cooked.

Serves 4

2 quinces

100g caster sugar, plus 45g

1 sprig of rosemary

4 tablespoons demerara sugar

50g non-dairy butter, plus extra for greasing

200ml oat cream

150ml non-dairy milk

seeds from 1 vanilla pod or ½ teaspoon vanilla paste

1 lemon, zested

45g caster sugar

45g plain flour

1 teaspoon baking powder

1 tablespoon icing sugar, for dusting

For the yogurt sorbet

100g caster sugar

25g agave syrup

200ml non-dairy milk

½ teaspoon xanthan gum

25ml vodka

zest and juice of 1 lemon

400g non-dairy yogurt

Begin by making the yogurt sorbet. Put the sugar and agave into a small saucepan with the milk and 100ml of water and bring to the boil. Once the sugar has dissolved, add the xanthan gum and whisk over the heat for 1 minute until thick. Remove from the heat and add the remaining ingredients. Whisk well, then freeze, whisking regularly to break up the ice crystals, or churn in an ice-cream maker following the manufacturer's instructions.

Peel the quinces, then cut into 12 wedges in total, removing the core. Put 100g of the caster sugar into a medium saucepan with the rosemary and 300ml water. Bring to the boil, then add the quinces, topping up with more water if required to completely submerge the fruit. Simmer gently for 40–45 minutes until the quinces are tender. Strain and pat dry with kitchen paper.

Preheat the oven to 180°C/fan 160°C/gas mark 4. Lightly grease a 20cm casserole with butter.

Put the demerara sugar in a small, heavy-based saucepan or frying pan. Set over a medium heat and leave the sugar to melt and caramelise to a deep golden colour, swirling the pan occasionally for even caramelisation. Add the butter, whisk well, and simmer for 1–2 minutes until well combined.

Pour the caramel into a casserole, then arrange the quince wedges on top.

Put the cream, milk, vanilla seeds and lemon zest in a small saucepan and bring gently to the boil. Remove from the heat.

In a deep bowl, whisk together the 45g of caster sugar, flour and baking powder, then add the hot cream mixture and combine well.

Pour the batter over the quince then place in the oven for about 15 minutes, until golden and cooked through. Dust with icing sugar and serve immediately with the yogurt sorbet.

Caramelised Banana Crème Brûlée,
Black Sesame Ice Cream, Cashews

This is a great recipe to use up any overripe bananas – the riper they are, the better the flavour. If you only have green bananas you will need to wait until brown spots appear on the skin, as this indicates that the starch has converted to sugar, so the fruit tastes sweeter and has a less solid structure.

Makes 6

For the ice cream

50g black sesame seeds, toasted

200ml non-dairy milk

100g caster sugar

50g tahini

250ml oat cream

50ml vodka

½ teaspoon xanthan gum

For the crème brûlée

80g demerara sugar

2 overripe bananas, peeled and roughly mashed

25ml dark rum

200ml oat cream

1 sachet Vege-Gel (vegan gelatine)

150ml coconut milk

100ml non-dairy milk

6 teaspoons caster sugar, for caramelising

For the cashews

1 tablespoon treacle

1 teaspoon sesame oil

2 tablespoons black sesame seeds, toasted

1 tablespoon demerara sugar

½ teaspoon sea salt flakes

60g cashew nuts

Begin by making the ice cream. Put the sesame seeds, milk and sugar in a small saucepan over a low heat and simmer for 10 minutes. Remove from the heat, cover and set aside for 10 minutes. Transfer to a blender with the tahini and cream and blend until smooth. Add the vodka and xanthan gum and blend for a further 3 minutes. Freeze, whisking regularly to break up the ice crystals, or churn in an ice-cream maker following the manufacturer's instructions.

For the crème brûlée, put the demerara sugar in a medium, heavy-based saucepan over a moderately high heat. Gently shake the pan when you see the sugar beginning to melt. Do not stir, as this may cause the caramel to crystallise. As it continues to melt, keep shaking and swirling the pan until a deep caramel is formed. Add the bananas and keep shaking the pan until they are covered with caramel. Add the rum and now begin to stir the caramel. Cook, while stirring, for at least 10 minutes until the mixture has combined and any lumps of banana have broken down. Stir in the cream, mix well, then blend until smooth. Put the gelatine into a separate pan with the coconut milk and milk and leave to sit for 10 minutes. Place over a medium heat, whisking well, and bring to the boil for 1 minute. Add to the banana mix, mix well, then pour through a fine sieve into six ramekins and refrigerate for at least 2 hours.

Preheat the oven to 170°C/fan 150°C/gas mark 3.

For the cashews, mix the treacle and sesame oil together, then add the other ingredients, coating the nuts well. Pour onto a baking tray lined with parchment paper and bake for 10–12 minutes until golden. Allow the nuts to cool, then roughly chop.

To serve, put a teaspoon of caster sugar onto each crème brûlée. Blow torch until caramelised, then top with the chopped nuts and a scoop of black sesame ice cream.

Apple Tarte Tatin
with Bay Leaf Ice Cream

Tarte Tatin has to be one of the best desserts ever created, and with only four ingredients it is so simple, but so delicious. I always use Pink Lady apples, which I peel and leave uncovered in the fridge for a day or two, so they dry out a little and hold their shape better when cooking. They will brown a little, but as they are being cooked it is not an issue. The bay leaves in this ice cream give it a slight savoury note, which works really well with the richness of the tatin.

Serves 4

80g non-dairy butter

80g caster sugar

4 Pink Lady apples, peeled, cored and halved

½ quantity of Puff Pastry (see page 182) or 1 sheet (320g) ready-rolled vegan puff pastry

For the ice cream

150ml coconut cream

100ml oat cream

200ml non-dairy milk

100g caster sugar

4 bay leaves

30ml vodka

½ teaspoon xanthan gum

For the ice cream, put the creams, milk, sugar and bay leaves into a medium saucepan over a medium heat. Bring to the boil for 4 minutes, then remove from the heat and blend using a stick blender. Cover with clingfilm and set aside for 20 minutes for the bay leaves to infuse. Strain through a fine sieve, add the vodka and xanthan gum and whisk for 3 minutes until the mixture begins to thicken. Freeze, whisking regularly to break up the ice crystals, or churn in an ice-cream maker following the manufacturer's instructions.

Preheat the oven to 180°C/fan 160°C/gas mark 4.

Spread the butter over the base of an 18cm ovenproof saucepan to form an even layer. Top with the caster sugar and shake to distribute evenly. Press the flat side of the halved apples into the butter and sugar around the outside of the saucepan – use 7 of the halves for the outside and set one, on its side, in the centre. Cut an 18cm circle out of the pastry and place on top of the apples. Set the saucepan over a medium heat until the butter has melted fully. Transfer the saucepan to the oven and bake for 35–40 minutes until the pastry is golden and a deep coloured caramel has formed.

Turn out the Tatin onto a serving plate and serve with the ice cream.

Baked Rice Puddings,
Winter Spice, Prune and Armagnac

Rice pudding is a classic dessert, one that was an occasional treat when I was growing up. When cooked well, it is a bowlful of sweet comfort. It is important to use pudding rice to make this as the grains are slightly fatter and take a little longer to cook, so they can absorb all of the spiced creamy milk. Do ensure the rice is cooked before serving though, as there is nothing worse than crunchy grains in what is supposed to be a creamy and soft pudding.

Serves 6

200ml coconut milk

200ml oat cream

600ml non-dairy milk

50g caster sugar

4 cardamom pods

2 star anise

½ nutmeg, finely grated

6 cloves

2 bay leaves

peel of ½ orange

50g non-dairy butter

1 tablespoon cornflour

150g pudding rice

For the prunes

50g caster sugar

1 teaspoon Earl Grey or English Breakfast tea leaves

100g pitted prunes

50ml Armagnac

non-dairy ice cream, to serve

Preheat the oven to 170°C/fan 150°C/gas mark 3.

Put the coconut milk, cream and milk into a medium saucepan with the sugar, spices, bay leaves and orange peel. Bring to a gentle simmer for 10 minutes, then turn off the heat and cover for a further 10 minutes to infuse. Using a stick blender, blend together. Strain through a fine sieve into a clean medium saucepan. Add the butter and cornflour and whisk well. Bring to a simmer and add the rice, stirring well. Pour into 6 ovenproof ramekins and bake for 1½ hours until golden on top.

Meanwhile, for the prunes, put the sugar and 250ml of water in a medium saucepan and bring to the boil. Add the tea leaves and boil for a further minute, then remove from the heat and allow to infuse for 10 minutes. Strain through a sieve into a clean saucepan and add the prunes and Armagnac. Bring to a gentle simmer for 10 minutes, then remove from the heat, cover and set aside until ready to use.

To serve, dollop the prunes on top of the rice puddings. Serve with a scoop of ice cream.

Pear and Ginger Cake,
Pine Nut Crème, Rosemary Caramel

Served warm, this is the ultimate winter comfort pudding. Use the ripest pears you can find to ensure the cake is deliciously moist. This cake also keeps very well, so can be made in advance and warmed up to serve. It is also perfect to have for afternoon tea on its own.

Serves 8

2 pears, peeled, cored and quartered
2 tablespoons golden syrup
pinch of table salt

For the pear and ginger cake
120g non-dairy butter
150g dark brown muscovado sugar
150g golden syrup
100g stem ginger, blitzed into a paste
½ nutmeg, grated
2 pears, peeled and grated
½ teaspoon bicarbonate of soda
250g self-raising flour

For the pine nut crème
100g pine nuts
pinch of table salt

For the rosemary caramel
125g caster sugar
1 teaspoon finely chopped rosemary leaves
100ml pear juice
50g butter
¼ teaspoon table salt
50ml oat cream

Preheat the oven to 170°C/fan 150°C/gas mark 3. Grease and line a 23cm square cake tin.

Arrange the quartered pears in a roasting dish. Drizzle with the golden syrup and sprinkle with the salt. Bake for 30–35 minutes until golden and soft.

For the pine nut crème, spread the pine nuts on a baking tray and roast in the hot oven for 8–10 minutes until golden. Place in a blender with the salt and 30ml of warm water. Blend until smooth and mousse-like, adding a little more water if necessary.

To make the cake, put the butter, sugar and golden syrup in a large bowl. Set over a medium saucepan half-filled with water, over a medium heat. Allow the butter to melt, then mix well. Add the ginger, nutmeg and grated pear, mix well. Stir in the bicarbonate of soda, then fold in the flour.

Pour the batter into the prepared cake tin. Bake for 30–35 minutes until a skewer inserted into the centre comes out clean. Cool in the tin for 10 minutes, then turn out onto a wire rack.

For the caramel, place the sugar and rosemary in a medium, heavy-based saucepan over a moderately high heat. Gently shake the pan when you see the sugar beginning to melt. Do not stir as this may cause the caramel to crystallise. As it continues to melt, keep shaking and swirling the pan until a deep caramel is formed. Add the pear juice and continue swirling the pan for 3 minutes. Add the butter and salt and swirl for 2 minutes. Finally, add the cream and whisk until a smooth caramel is formed.

To serve, slice the warm cake into 8 pieces. Top with the caramel and pine nut cream. Serve with 2 pieces of roasted pear.

Dark Chocolate Mousse,
Cocoa Nibs, Passion Fruit and Chamomile

Chocolate mousse is one of life's simple pleasures. Paired with the toasted crunch of cocoa nibs, the acidity of fresh passion fruit makes it even more so. The chamomile adds a little floral touch, and the meringue gives a wonderfully light texture. This mousse can be made in advance.

Serves 8

150g aquafaba

80g caster sugar

½ teaspoon xanthan gum

150g dark chocolate, minimum 70% cocoa solids, broken into pieces

100ml coconut cream

100ml oat cream

For the chamomile jelly

2 tablespoons caster sugar

zest and juice of 1 lemon

2 tablespoons chamomile tea flowers

½ sachet Vege-Gel (vegan gelatine)

For the cocoa nibs

40g caster sugar

¼ teaspoon chamomile tea flowers

60g toasted cocoa nibs

3 passion fruit, pulp scooped out, to serve

Start by making the jelly. Put the sugar, lemon zest and juice in a saucepan with 150ml of warm water and bring to the boil. Remove from the heat, add the chamomile tea and leave to infuse for 10 minutes. Strain through a fine sieve into a clean pan and sprinkle the Vege-Gel on top. Leave to sit for 5 minutes then place back on the heat and bring to the boil, continuously whisking. Boil for 3 minutes, then pour through a fine sieve into a clean container. Refrigerate until set.

For the cocoa nibs, put the sugar and chamomile into a small, heavy-based saucepan over a moderately high heat. Gently shake the pan when you see the sugar beginning to melt. Do not stir as this may cause the caramel to crystallise. As it continues to melt, keep shaking and swirling the pan until a deep caramel is formed. Add the cocoa nibs and mix well. Remove from the heat and spread, as thinly as possible, on a silicone mat or a baking tray greased with a little oil. Allow to cool, then finely chop.

Meanwhile, whisk the aquafaba in a bowl with an electric whisk, or using a stand mixer, until stiff. Gradually add the sugar, then continue whisking for up to 10 minutes until glossy and thick. Add the xanthan gum and whisk for a further 3 minutes on a high speed.

While the meringue is whisking, put the chocolate in a medium bowl over a small saucepan half-filled with water. Set the pan over a moderately high heat until the water is gently simmering. Stir the chocolate until it has completely melted and no lumps remain. Put the creams in a small saucepan and bring to the boil. Transfer the bowl of chocolate to the worktop and pour in the hot cream. Whisk well, then gently fold the meringue into the chocolate and spoon into a large bowl. Cover and refrigerate for 20 minutes.

To serve, roughly chop the caramelised cocoa nibs. Scatter on 8 plates, then divide the passionfruit pulp and jelly between the plates. Finish with a large scoop of the chocolate mousse.

Gin and Elderflower Cheesecakes

I have a slight 'thing' of making desserts from cocktails, or from my favourite drinks. Here, it is a take on a good old gin and tonic. As with anything you cook, it is important to start with good-quality and tasty ingredients. Try your favourite gin in this one, it will not disappoint.

Makes 6

For the cheesecakes
250g non-dairy cream cheese
150g non-dairy cream
zest and juice of 1 lemon
25g caster sugar
25ml gin
30ml elderflower cordial
¾ sachet Vege-Gel (vegan gelatine)

For the jelly
100ml tonic water
35ml gin
1 tablespoon elderflower cordial
¼ sachet Vege-Gel (vegan gelatine)

½ quantity of Almond Crumb

Line six 6 x 4cm ring moulds with clingfilm.

Put the cream cheese, 50g of the cream, lemon zest and juice and sugar in a blender and blend until smooth. Put the remaining cream in a saucepan with the gin and elderflower cordial. Add the Vege-Gel and soak for 10 minutes. Bring to the boil for 1 minute, whisking continuously, then add to the cream cheese mix. Blend well, then pour into the ring moulds. Refrigerate for 2 hours or until set.

Once the cheesecakes are set, put all jelly ingredients into a small saucepan with 25ml of water. Whisk well and let sit for 10 minutes. Bring to the boil, remove from the heat then pour over the cheesecakes. Refrigerate for 1 hour, or until set.

To assemble, finely break up the almond crumb. Divide into 6 and using a 6 x 4cm ring mould, press the crumb into the bottom, to form a neat circle. Remove the clingfilm from the bottom of a cheesecake and place directly on top of the crumb. Using a blow torch, or your hands, warm the ring so the cheesecake slips out. Repeat with the other five cheesecakes.

Almond Crumb

75g non-dairy butter
100g demerara sugar
180g plain flour
50g ground almonds

Beat together the butter and sugar. Mix in the flour and almonds. Cover in clingfilm and rest for 20 minutes.

To bake, preheat the oven to 180°C/fan 160°C/gas mark 4. Break up the mixture and place on a silicone mat or piece of parchment paper, on a baking tray. Bake for 12–15 minutes, stirring every few minutes until a crumb is formed.

Remove from the oven and allow to cool.

Cherry and Earl Grey Tart

Earl Grey tea is flavoured with bergamot, a citrus fruit that has a wonderfully aromatic scent. The flavour profile works really well with the cherries in this recipe. Cherries have very fond childhood memories for me, as my aunt and uncle have a stone fruit orchard in Central Otago in NZ.

Serves 8

For the pastry

175g plain flour, plus extra for dusting

50g caster sugar

pinch of sea salt

115g non-dairy butter

50ml non-dairy milk

2 tablespoons aquafaba

For the custard

150ml non-dairy cream

150ml non-dairy milk

50g caster sugar

2 tablespoons custard powder

300g cherries, halved and stoned

For the Earl Grey jelly

100g caster sugar

1 tablespoon Earl Grey tea leaves

½ sachet Vege-Gel (vegan gelatine)

25ml kirsch

Grease and line a 23cm loose-bottom tart tin.

To make the pastry, rub together the flour, sugar, salt and butter in a bowl, or process in a food processor until the mixture resembles breadcrumbs. Gradually add the milk to form a soft, pliable dough. Wrap the dough in clingfilm and chill for 30 minutes.

Roll out the pastry on a lightly floured surface to make a round large enough to fit in the tart tin. Transfer to the lined tin, leaving a little excess pastry to hang over the edges. Return to the fridge for 20 minutes.

Meanwhile, preheat the oven to 190°C/fan 170°/gas mark 5.

When the pastry has rested, line it with baking parchment and fill with baking beans. Transfer the tart case to the oven and bake for 20 minutes, until it starts to turn a light golden colour. Remove the baking beans and parchment, brush with the aquafaba and return the case to the oven for a further 5 minutes. Remove from the oven and allow to cool slightly. When cool enough to handle, trim away the excess pastry with a sharp knife.

For the custard, put the cream and milk in a saucepan and bring to the boil. Put the sugar and custard powder into a bowl and mix well. Pour a little of the hot cream into the sugar mix and whisk well. Add this mix to the saucepan and whisk well. Place over a low heat and stir constantly until the mixture has thickened. Pour into the cooled tart case.

Arrange the cherries, cut-side down, on top of the custard.

For the jelly, pour 250ml of water into a pan, add the sugar and bring to the boil. Add the tea and Vege-Gel, whisk well and leave to sit for 10 minutes. Whisk well then strain through a fine sieve. Stir in the kirsch, allow the jelly to cool slightly then pour over the top of the cherries.

Refrigerate the tart for at least 2 hours until set.

Rhubarb Panna Cotta,
Poached Rhubarb, Warm Almond Cakes

Rhubarb is such favourite of mine. I love the forced rhubarb for its wonderful vibrant pink hue. But the outdoor rhubarb has so much flavour, so in the UK we get the best of both worlds. The grenadine works as a flavour enhancer and also creates the beautiful pink hue.

Serves 6

For the panna cotta

300g rhubarb, finely chopped

100g caster sugar

2 tablespoons grenadine

150ml non-dairy milk

250ml coconut milk

¾ sachet Vege-Gel (vegan gelatine)

For the rhubarb

100g caster sugar

2 tablespoons grenadine

200g rhubarb, sliced into 10cm pieces

¼ sachet Vege-Gel (vegan gelatine)

For the almond cakes

65g ground almonds

2 tablespoons plain flour

90g caster sugar

30g aquafaba

65g non-dairy butter, plus extra for greasing

To decorate

edible flowers

icing sugar

For the panna cotta put the rhubarb, sugar, grenadine and 100ml water into a medium saucepan over a medium heat. Bring to a simmer and cook until the rhubarb has broken down and formed a purée. Add the non-dairy milk and coconut milk and blend with a stick blender until smooth. Strain through a fine sieve into a saucepan, add the Vege-Gel and bring to a rapid simmer for 2 minutes. Pour into 6 glasses and refrigerate for at least 2 hours.

To make the poached rhubarb, put the sugar, grenadine and 300ml water in a large saucepan and bring to the boil. Turn down the heat to a gentle simmer and add the rhubarb. This should be in a single layer on the base of the pan. Simmer very gently for 3–5 minutes until the rhubarb is almost soft to touch. Remove the rhubarb from the cooking liquor and refrigerate immediately, to stop it cooking any further. Bring the cooking liquor to the boil and boil for 5 minutes. Add the Vege-Gel, whisk well, and boil for a further 3 minutes. Strain through a fine sieve into a container approximately 20 x 15cm and refrigerate until set.

Preheat the oven to 180°C/fan 160°C/gas mark 4. Lightly grease a 12-hole non-stick muffin tin with oil.

To make the almond cakes, mix the ground almonds and flour together. Add the sugar and aquafaba and whisk together to combine. Melt the butter in a small saucepan over a high heat, then slowly pour this into the almond mixture, blending as you pour.

Spoon the cake mixture into the holes of the tin. Take two sticks of the rhubarb from the fridge and cut each into six pieces. Pop a piece on top of each almond cake. Bake for 15 minutes until golden and firm to the touch.

Remove the cakes from the tin immediately and place on a wire rack to cool. When ready to serve, cut the poached rhubarb pieces and using a hot knife, cut the rhubarb jelly into cubes. Top the panna cottas with some of the fruit and jelly and decorate with a few edible flowers. Serve with the almond cakes (they are nicest slightly warmed in a low oven), dusted with icing sugar.

Peaches, Meringue,
Cream Cheese Frosting and Tarragon

This pudding is similar to an Eton Mess, with broken meringue, fruit and cream. You can substitute the peaches for any stone fruit, with greengage plums being one a particular favourite of mine. The cream cheese frosting can also be used for other desserts, and also to decorate cakes.

Serves 8

¼ bunch of tarragon, leaves and stalks separated, a few reserved to garnish

200g caster sugar

100ml white wine

pinch of saffron strands

¼ teaspoon fennel seeds

2 bay leaves

zest and juice of 1 lemon

4 peaches, halved and stoned

For the meringue

60g aquafaba

120g caster sugar

For the cream cheese frosting

25g non-dairy butter

50g non-dairy cream cheese

25g icing sugar, sifted

zest of ½ lemon

Put the tarragon stalks, sugar, wine, saffron, fennel seeds, bay leaves, lemon zest and juice in a large saucepan. Top with 400ml water and bring to the boil. Reduce to a very gentle simmer and add all but one of the halved peaches. Cover with a lid or a circle of parchment paper, and cook for 25–35 minutes until the peaches are soft and the skin peels away easily.

Remove the peaches from the cooking liquor using a slotted spoon and place on a tray to cool. When cool enough to handle, peel the skin off gently. Refrigerate until cold, then slice each half into four.

Return the cooking liquor to a high heat and reduce by two-thirds, until a thick syrup is formed. Strain and set aside to cool. When cold, add the tarragon leaves, reserving a few for decoration.

Preheat the oven to 100°C/fan 80°C/gas mark ¼. Line a tray with parchment paper. Whisk the aquafaba in a bowl with an electric whisk, or using a stand mixer, until stiff. Continue whisking and gradually add the sugar. Whisk until the meringue is glossy and all sugar grains have dissolved.

Spread the meringue onto the lined tray and put in the oven for 30 minutes or until crisp on the outside. Turn the oven off and leave the door ajar until the meringue has cooled.

For the frosting, put the butter and cream cheese in a bowl and whisk until smooth. Add the icing sugar and zest and whisk until combined.

To assemble, arrange the peach wedges on plates, drizzling liberally with the syrup. Pipe or spoon the frosting around the peaches and cut the reserved fresh peach half into very thin slices, looping them around the poached peaches. Decorate with broken up meringue and tarragon leaves.

Palm Sugar and Rum-roasted Pineapple, Coconut, Lime and Mint

Whole roasted pineapple, basted with palm sugar and rum is a pretty hard thing to beat. Ensure you use the ripest pineapple you can find. I would recommend buying one a few days in advance of needing to use it, and leaving it in your fruit bowl to ensure it reaches maximum ripeness. The outside skin should be golden not green or pale yellow.

Serves 4

100g palm sugar, finely grated
100ml dark rum
½ nutmeg, finely grated
½ teaspoon table salt
1 pineapple, skinned

For the coconut mousse

140g caster sugar
70g aquafaba
250g coconut yogurt
25ml coconut liqueur
zest and juice of 1 lime

small mint leaves, to garnish

Preheat the oven to 180°C/fan 160°C/gas mark 4.

Put the palm sugar in a medium frying pan over a medium heat. Gently shake the pan when you see the sugar beginning to melt. Do not stir, as this may cause the caramel to crystallise. As it continues to melt, keep shaking and swirling the pan until a medium coloured caramel is formed. Add the rum and whisk well. Boil for 3 minutes, then add the nutmeg and salt.

Place the pineapple in a roasting dish and brush liberally with the rum caramel. Roast for 60 minutes, basting every 8–10 minutes with the rum caramel.

Remove from the oven and transfer the pineapple from the roasting dish to a plate, covering it with foil to keep warm. Pour the cooking juices into a saucepan and bring to the boil. Reduce until a caramel is formed. Keep warm.

For the coconut mousse, put the sugar and 3 tablespoons water in a small saucepan and set over low–medium heat. Stir until the sugar dissolves, then bring to a fast boil, until it reaches 121°C on a sugar thermometer.

Meanwhile, whisk the aquafaba in a bowl with an electric whisk, or using a standmixer, until stiff. When the syrup temperature reaches 121°C on the sugar thermometer, slowly and carefully pour the syrup over the aquafaba in a thin stream while continuing to whisk. Continue whisking for up to 10 minutes until the meringue has cooled.

Whisk together the coconut yogurt, coconut liqueur, lime zest and juice. Fold in the meringue.

Carve the pineapple into 8 slices and drizzle liberally with the caramel. Serve with the coconut mousse on the side and garnish with the mint leaves.

Lemon Meringue Tarts,
Black Olive Caramel

The black olive in this dish brings a depth of savouriness that cuts through the sweetness of the other elements. It is a great thing to have on hand for other puddings too. You will need to dehydrate the olives overnight though, so plan ahead.

Serves 8

For the black olive caramel

50g pitted black olives, halved

80g caster sugar

For the sweet pastry

45g non-dairy butter

55g caster sugar

110g plain flour, plus extra for dusting

½ teaspoon baking powder

¼ teaspoon table salt

30ml oat cream

For the meringue

70g aquafaba

140g caster sugar

50g coconut yogurt

30g non-dairy cream

½ teaspoon xanthan gum

1 quantity of Lemon Curd (see page 184)

To dehydrate the olives, preheat the oven to 70°C/fan 50°C/gas mark ¼, or to its lowest setting. Put the olives on baking tray and leave in the oven for 6–8 hours until completely dry. Reserve 10g, then blend the rest in a small blender until the oil begins to come out of the olives, forming a smooth paste.

Lay a large piece of greased parchment paper on your worktop. Put the sugar in a medium, heavy-based saucepan over a moderately high heat. Gently shake the pan when you see the sugar beginning to melt. Keep shaking as it continues to melt, swirling the pan until a medium coloured caramel is formed. Add the olive paste and whisk well. Quickly turn out onto half the greased parchment paper. Fold over the other half of the paper and, using a rolling pin, roll out to a very thin layer. Cool, then snap into shards.

For the sweet pastry, put the butter and sugar into a bowl and beat until pale and creamy. Add the flour, baking powder and salt and mix well. Add the cream and mix until a smooth dough is formed. Wrap in clingfilm and refrigerate for 20 minutes.

Preheat the oven to 170°C/fan 150°C/gas mark 3 and line a baking tray with parchment paper. Roll out the pastry on a floured surface into a 2mm thick rectangle. Place on the prepared baking tray and chill for 10 minutes. Bake for 8 minutes, then remove from the oven and cut 16 rectangles. Bake, uncovered, for a further 6–8 minutes until pale golden.

For the meringues, whisk the aquafaba until thick. Gradually add the caster sugar, bit by bit, then whisk on full speed for 10–12 minutes, until glossy and no sugar grains remain. Pipe small meringues onto parchment paper, and sprinkle with the remaining black olive, finely chopped. Place into the oven for 30 minutes, until crispy on the outside.

Whisk the yogurt and cream together with the xanthan gum until thick.

To assemble, pipe or spoon the lemon curd onto the pastry rectangles and garnish with the meringues and black olive caramel.

Apricot Frangipane Tart

Sweet and ripe apricots also take me back to my aunt and uncles orchard in New Zealand. Apricot were always my favourite fruit to eat there and my uncle grew the best ones we ever tasted – picked straight from the tree, lightly warmed by the summer sun.

Serves 8

For the pastry

175g plain flour, plus extra for dusting
50g caster sugar
pinch of sea salt
115g non-dairy butter
50ml non-dairy milk
2 tablespoons aquafaba

For the frangipane

150g caster sugar
150g non-dairy butter
100g aquafaba
pinch of sea salt
200g ground almonds

4 tablespoons apricot jam
8 ripe apricots, halved, stoned and sliced into 6
25ml almond liqueur

To make the pastry, rub together the flour, sugar, salt and butter in a bowl, or process in a food processor until the mixture resembles breadcrumbs. Gradually add the milk to form a soft, pliable dough. Wrap the dough in clingfilm and chill for 30 minutes.

Roll out the pastry on a lightly floured surface to a thickness of 3mm and use it to line a greased, 23cm loose-bottomed tart tin, on a baking tray lined with parchment paper, leaving a little excess pastry to hang over the edges. Return to the fridge for 20 minutes.

Meanwhile, preheat the oven to 190°C/fan 170°C/gas mark 5.

Line the pastry case with baking parchment and fill with baking beans. Bake for 20 minutes, until the pastry starts to turn a light golden colour. Remove the baking beans and parchment, brush with the aquafaba and return the case to the oven for a further 5 minutes. Remove from the oven and allow to cool slightly. When cool enough to handle, trim away the excess pastry with a sharp knife. Reduce the oven temperature to 180°C/fan 160°C/gas mark 4.

To make the frangipane, beat together the sugar and butter in a bowl until light and creamy. Add the aquafaba and beat well. Mix in the salt and ground almonds.

Spread 3 tablespoons of the apricot jam over the base of the pastry case, then top with the frangipane. Smooth the top then arrange the sliced apricots on top, in a circular manner, to cover all the tart. Bake for 40–45 minutes, until the tart is deep golden and the frangipane has just set in the centre. Remove from the oven and leave to cool for at least 10 minutes in the tin.

While the tart is cooling, whisk the remaining jam together with the almond liqueur. Liberally brush the top of the tart a few times with this syrup, then remove from the tin and allow to cool completely on a wire rack. Serve with ice cream or yogurt.

Flapjack-baked Figs
with Thyme and Sesame

This is one of my favourite ways to serve figs – lightly baked in the oven with the spiced flapjack makes for a pudding all in one. You can use black or green figs, just ensure they are as ripe as can be. Underripe figs can be a little bitter and lack the sweetness of a perfectly ripened one. I serve these with coconut yogurt and a non-dairy vanilla ice cream.

Serves 4

85g non-dairy butter
30g demerara sugar
40g golden syrup
65g rolled oats
20g sesame seeds
½ teaspoon ground cinnamon
1 teaspoon thyme leaves
½ teaspoon table salt

8 large figs

non-dairy vanilla ice cream or coconut yogurt, to serve

Preheat the oven to 180°C/fan 160°C/gas mark 4.

Put the butter, sugar and golden syrup in a small saucepan. Heat until the sugar has dissolved and the mixture has combined. Mix the rolled oats, sesame seeds, cinnamon, thyme and salt together, then add butter mixture and stir until combined.

Carefully slice the top of each fig to form an X, ensuring you only slice halfway down the fig. Stuff the incision with some of the flapjack mix and place on a tray. Bake for 10 minutes. Roll the remaining flapjack mix between two sheets of baking paper, transfer to another tray and cook for 5–8 minutes until crispy.

Serve the baked figs with pieces of the flapjack and a good dollop of non-dairy ice cream or coconut yogurt.

Strawberries, Basil, Tequila Ice,
Toasted Black Pepper Crème

Again, this may sound like an 'interesting' combination, but trust me, it works so well when you need something refreshing and cooling on a hot summer's day. Select strawberries that are deep red with a heady scent, as they will be sweeter and more flavoursome.

Serves 6

For the tequila ice

150g caster sugar
100ml reposado (aged) tequila
zest and juice of 1 lime

For the basil and lemon sauce

1 bunch of basil, leaves only
100g caster sugar
zest and juice of 2 lemons

For the toasted black pepper crème

160g caster sugar
80g aquafaba
1 teaspoon ground black pepper
100ml oat cream
100g coconut yogurt

800g strawberries, hulled and halved
micro basil, to serve

First make the tequila ice. Put the sugar in a saucepan with 200ml of water, bring to the boil and stir until the sugar has dissolved. Add another 300ml of cold water, the tequila and lime zest and juice. Whisk until combined then place in a freezerproof container and place in the freezer. Whisk every 20 minutes until frozen, then scrape with a fork to form a soft ice.

For the basil and lemon sauce, place all the ingredients into a jug or beaker and blend together using a stick blender, then refrigerate until serving.

To make the toasted black pepper crème, put the sugar and 3 tablespoons of water in a small saucepan and set over low–medium heat. Stir until the sugar dissolves, then bring to a fast boil, until it reaches 121°C on a sugar thermometer.

Meanwhile, whisk the aquafaba in a bowl with an electric whisk, or using a standmixer, until stiff. When the syrup temperature reaches 121°C on the sugar thermometer, slowly and carefully pour the syrup over the aquafaba in a thin stream while continuing to whisk. Continue whisking for up to 10 minutes, until the meringue has cooled.

While the meringue is whisking, put the pepper into a medium saucepan over a moderately high heat. Toast until fragrant, then add the oat cream and remove from the heat. Allow to infuse for 10 minutes. Pour into a mixing bowl and add the coconut yogurt, mixing well. Fold in the meringue.

Place six bowls in the freezer for at least 20 minutes before serving. To serve, remove the bowls from the freezer and place the tequila ice in the bottom. Top with the basil sauce, strawberries, black pepper crème and micro basil.

Bakes

Raspberry and Rose Muffins

Raspberry and rose flavour profiles work really well together. The rose in this recipe is subtle, but if you are not a fan you can leave it out. These muffins freeze well so you can make a batch and pop what you don't eat on the day into the freezer. Warm them a little when they have defrosted for the best result.

Makes 12 muffins

375g plain flour

4½ teaspoons baking powder

170g caster sugar

1 tablespoon rose water

75g coconut cream

100ml non-dairy milk

75g non-dairy butter, melted, plus a little extra for greasing

150g raspberries

6 teaspoons raspberry jam

1 tablespoon dried rose petals

icing sugar, for dusting

Preheat the oven to 170°C/fan 150°C/gas mark 3. Grease a 12-hole muffin tin.

Put the flour, baking powder and sugar in a large bowl and mix well. Form a well in the centre. In a separate bowl, mix the rose water, cream, milk and melted butter together and pour into the centre of the dry ingredients. Add the raspberries, then gently fold everything together, being careful not to overmix.

Spoon half the muffin batter into the greased muffin tin. Place ½ a teaspoonful of raspberry jam on top of the batter in each muffin hole. Cover with the remaining batter and sprinkle with the rose petals.

Bake for 20–25 minutes until lightly golden and a skewer inserted into the cake part comes out clean. Allow to cool for 10 minutes in the tin, then turn out and dust with icing sugar before serving.

Cornbread

Cornbread is a super versatile bake. It is delicious on its own, but also great to use as a garnish, and to have as a side with a bowl of soup. This recipe is quite spicy due to the jalapeños, so if you do not enjoy too much heat, reduce the quantity.

200g coarse cornmeal, preferably stoneground

100ml coconut milk

120ml non-dairy milk

50g non-dairy butter

100g sweetcorn kernels, tinned or frozen, blended

1 tablespoon soft dark brown sugar

½ teaspoon table salt

1 teaspoon baking powder

½ teaspoon bicarbonate of soda

100g aquafaba

30g green jalapeños, finely chopped

80g Cheddar-style non-dairy cheese, grated

Preheat the oven to 200°C/fan 180°C/gas mark 6.

Spread out the cornmeal in a roasting tray and place in the oven for 10 minutes. Remove and tip into a large mixing bowl and add the milks. Mix well and leave to soak for 10 minutes.

Put the butter in an 18 x 9cm (1lb) loaf tin. Place in the oven for 6 minutes.

Add the remaining ingredients to the soaked cornmeal. Remove the loaf tin from the oven and tip the hot butter into the mixture and stir well to combine.

Pour the batter into the tin. Bake for 25 minutes until a skewer inserted into the centre comes out clean. Remove the cornbread from the tin and cool on a wire rack.

Brioche

I love brioche and the challenge I set myself for this recipe was to create the same buttery texture and flavour created when you use dairy, butter and eggs. This final result works fantastically well.

350g plain flour

15g fresh yeast, or 5g fast-action dried yeast

15g caster sugar

1 teaspoon table salt

80g aquafaba

100ml coconut milk

50ml non-dairy milk

100g non-dairy butter

1 teaspoon olive oil, for greasing

Put the flour in a stand mixer bowl or a large mixing bowl. Keeping them in separate places on the flour, add the yeast, sugar and salt. Pour the aquafaba and milks into the centre of the flour and mix together, using a dough hook on your stand mixer on a low speed, or a firm wooden spoon, to form a smooth dough. When the dough is combined increase the mixer speed until the mixture leaves the sides of the bowl. If doing by hand, knead on your worktop until the dough loses all its stickiness.

Add the butter and work in until completely mixed into the dough. Work until the dough leaves the sides of the bowl again.

Place the dough in an oiled bowl and cover with clingfilm. Leave in a warm place to double in size.

Gently tip onto a lightly floured worktop and form into a loaf shape. Place in a greased 18 x 9cm (1lb) loaf tin and cover with clingfilm. Leave in a warm place to prove, again until doubled in size.

Preheat the oven to 175°C/fan 155°C/gas mark 3½ while the dough is proving for the second time.

Bake for 20–25 minutes until golden and a skewer inserted into the centre comes out clean. Tip out of the loaf tin and leave to cool on a wire rack.

Black Olive, Thyme and Onion Jam Rolls

These rolls are rather moreish, so they may not last more than a day. If you are not a fan of olives you can leave them out or replace with sundried tomatoes or capers. The rolls freeze very well too, just defrost, then pop into a hot oven for a few minutes prior to serving.

Makes 12 rolls

500g strong white flour, plus extra for dusting

23g fresh yeast, or 7g sachet fast-action dried yeast

1 tablespoon caster sugar

2 teaspoons table salt, plus extra for seasoning

50ml olive oil, plus extra for greasing

1 quantity of Onion Jam (see page 184)

80g Kalamata olives, pitted and finely chopped

1 tablespoon thyme leaves

Mix together the flour, yeast, sugar, salt, oil and 275ml of warm water in a bowl to form a soft, smooth dough that leaves the sides of the bowl. This can be done by hand or using a stand mixer fitted with a dough hook. Knead for about 10 minutes, until dough is smooth.

Lightly oil the inside of a bowl, place the dough into it and cover with lightly oiled clingfilm. Leave in a warm place for about 1 hour, or until the dough has doubled in size.

Tip the dough out onto a floured worktop and roll it into a large rectangle, about 1cm thick. Spread the onion jam over the dough, leaving a 4cm border on one long edge of the dough. Top with the olives and thyme leaves. Carefully roll the dough in on itself, leaving the border exposed. Brush the border with warm water then fold over the top of the dough. Turn the bread over so that the border seal is underneath. Cut the roll into 8 slices and place each piece cut-side up on an oiled baking tray. Cover with clingfilm and place in a warm place to prove for 30 minutes.

Preheat the oven to 170°C/fan 150°C/gas mark 3.

Remove the clingfilm and bake the rolls for 16–20 minutes until golden and cooked through. Serve warm.

Almond, Pear and Rosemary Friands

Friands are small almond cakes of French origin. They are typically oval in shape, but you can use any appropriate moulds you have. The rosemary in this recipe really gives the cakes a lift. If the pears are too wet, the friand mix will be too moist, hence needing to squeeze any excess juice.

Makes 12 friands

190g caster sugar

50g self-raising flour

125g ground almonds

1 tablespoon rosemary leaves, finely chopped

2 pears, peeled and grated, any excess moisture squeezed out

170g aquafaba

125g non-dairy butter, melted, plus extra for greasing

Preheat the oven to 170°C/fan 150°C/gas mark 3. Grease a 12-hole friand mould or muffin tin.

Put the sugar, flour, almonds and rosemary into a large mixing bowl. Add the pears and aquafaba and mix well. Gradually mix in the melted butter, in stages, until it has all been incorporated.

Divide the mix between the moulds and bake for 12–15 minutes until golden and a skewer inserted into the centre comes out clean. Remove from the moulds immediately and allow to cool on a wire rack.

Courgette, Tarragon and Black Pepper Scones

Scones were something I often baked at the weekends when I was growing up in New Zealand. They would either be date scones or savoury scones, which I used to trial a number of different vegetables and cheeses. These are delicious on their own, but also go well with soups and salads for a more substantial meal.

Makes 6 scones

2 courgettes, grated

2½ teaspoons table salt

250g self-raising flour, plus extra for dusting

3 tablespoons chopped tarragon leaves

75g non-dairy butter, frozen then grated

100g Cheddar-style non-dairy cheese, grated

1 teaspoon freshly milled black pepper

1 small onion, peeled and finely diced

100ml non-dairy milk

Put the grated courgette in a colander and sprinkle with 2 teaspoons of the salt. Set over a bowl and leave for 30 minutes to drain.

Put the courgettes in a clean tea towel and squeeze out as much of the liquid as possible.

Preheat the oven to 170°C/fan 150°C/gas mark 3 and lightly flour a baking tray.

Put the flour, remaining salt and tarragon in a bowl and rub in the butter until the mixture resembles breadcrumbs. Mix in half the cheese, the black pepper and onion. Slowly add the milk, mixing just enough to bring together into a firm dough, taking care not to overmix.

Roll out the dough on a floured worktop to 5cm thick. Cover loosely with clingfilm and leave to rest for 10 minutes before cutting into 6 squares.

Transfer to the baking tray and sprinkle with the remaining grated cheese and extra black pepper. Bake for 20–25 minutes until the scones are golden and cooked through.

Maple, Cinnamon and Raisin Buns

These are like a cross between a *pain aux raisins* and a Chelsea bun. They are a perfect winter treat with a good cup of coffee. If you can find the larger, sticky 'Flame' raisins they have a more intense flavour. Heralding from the red, seedless, Flame grape, they are classified as the sweetest raisin.

Makes 8 buns

For the dough

500g strong white flour, plus extra for dusting

1 teaspoon table salt

20g fresh yeast or 7g sachet fast-action dried yeast

200ml non-dairy milk

50ml maple syrup

50g non-dairy butter, plus extra for greasing

50ml aquafaba

100g raisins, preferably Flame

60g non-dairy butter, melted

50g maple syrup, plus extra for drizzling

1 tablespoon soft brown sugar

1 tablespoon ground cinnamon

½ teaspoon sea salt

First soak the raisins. Put in a bowl and cover with boiling water. Set aside for 30 minutes, then drain.

To make the dough, mix together the flour, salt and yeast in a large bowl or stand mixer. Add the remaining ingredients and mix to form a soft, smooth dough that leaves the sides of the bowl. This can be done by hand or using a stand mixer fitted with a dough hook. Knead for about 10 minutes until the dough is smooth.

Lightly oil a bowl, place the dough inside and cover with lightly oiled clingfilm. Leave somewhere warm for about 1 hour, or until the dough has doubled in size.

Once the dough has risen, whisk the melted butter with the maple syrup, sugar, cinnamon and sea salt.

Tip the bread dough out onto a floured worktop and roll it into a large rectangle, about 1cm thick. Leaving a 4cm border on one long edge of the dough, spread the maple butter onto the dough. Top with the raisins. Carefully roll the bread in on itself, leaving the border exposed. Brush the border with warm water, then fold over the top of the dough. Turn the bread over so that the border seal is underneath. Cut the roll into 8 slices and place, cut side up, on a greased baking tray. Cover with clingfilm and put in a warm place to prove for 30 minutes.

Preheat the oven to 170°C/fan 150°C/gas mark 3.

Remove the clingfilm and bake the rolls for 16–20 minutes until golden and cooked through. Serve warm with a further drizzle of maple syrup.

Lavender and Lime Drizzle Cake

Lavender, when used subtly, can be a great addition to cakes and baking. It needs to lightly perfume, rather than overpower though. Fresh is always best, but if not available, dried lavender will work in this case. This cake does need to be cooked in a ring tin, so if you do not have a fluted one, then a plain one will work just as well.

Serves 8

100g aquafaba

175g caster sugar

½ teaspoon xanthan gum

150g non-dairy butter, plus extra for greasing

zest of 1 lime

1 tablespoon lavender flowers, plus extra to garnish

200g self-raising flour

1 teaspoon baking powder

For the drizzle

zest and juice of 2 limes

50g caster sugar

40g demerara sugar, to finish

Preheat the oven to 165°C/fan 145°C/gas mark 3. Grease a 20 cm fluted ring tin.

Whisk the aquafaba in a bowl with an electric whisk, or using a standmixer, until stiff. Continue whisking and gradually add the caster sugar, then whisk until stiff and glossy. Add the xanthan gum and whisk for a further 3 minutes.

Soften the butter and beat until creamy. Add the lime zest and half of the lavender. Beat in the aquafaba in 3 stages. Mix the flour and baking powder together, the fold into the butter mix until just combined.

Scrape the batter into the prepared ring tin and bake for 25–30 minutes until a skewer inserted into the centre comes out clean. Prick the surface of the cake all over with a skewer, to create 'channels' for the syrup.

Allow to cool in the tin for 15 minutes, then turn the cake out.

Put the rest of the lavender flowers, lime zest and juice and caster sugar in a small saucepan with 1 tablespoon of water. Bring to the boil for 3 minutes, then gently pour over the cake. Sprinkle with the demerara sugar and extra lavender flowers and allow to cool.

Basics

Light Vegetable Stock

2 onions, peeled and quartered

3 carrots, peeled and halved

2 celery stalks, halved

1 leek, trimmed and cut into four

1 whole garlic bulb, halved horizontally

2 bay leaves

6 sprigs of thyme

6 peppercorns

¼ teaspoon coriander seeds

Put all the ingredients in a large saucepan with 6 litres of water. Bring to a simmer and cook gently for 2 hours. Strain and store the liquid in the fridge for up to five days, or freeze in batches.

Roasted Vegetable Stock

2 tablespoons vegetable oil

4 onions, roots removed and halved

1 leek, trimmed and cut into four

3 carrots, peeled and halved

2 celery stalks, halved

1 whole garlic bulb, halved horizontally

2 tablespoons tomato paste

½ teaspoon Marmite

2 sprigs of rosemary

2 bay leaves

4 sprigs of thyme

6 white peppercorns

½ teaspoon coriander seeds

½ teaspoon fennel seeds

Heat the vegetable oil in a large saucepan over a high heat. When almost smoking, add the onions, leek, carrots and celery and brown well. Add the garlic and brown for 2 minutes. Stir in the tomato paste and Marmite and mix well. Add 8 litres of water followed by the remaining ingredients. Turn down the heat and simmer gently for 2 hours. Strain off and refrigerate the liquid for up to five days, or freeze in batches.

Chickpea Chips

100g gram (chickpea) flour

30g yellow, quick cook polenta

¼ teaspoon toasted cumin seeds, finely crushed

50g canned chickpeas

1 tablespoon sesame oil

1 tablespoon tahini

1 teaspoon table salt

½ teaspoon ground black pepper

2 tablespoons flat-leaf parsley, finely chopped

plain flour, for dusting

vegetable oil, for deep frying

Line a 23cm square cake tin with clingfilm.

Put all the ingredients, apart from the parsley, in a medium saucepan. Mix together then whisk in 400ml cold water.

Set the pan over a medium heat and cook, stirring frequently, for 10–15 minutes, until the mix begins to leave the sides of the pan. Stir in the parsley then pour the mixture into the cake tin. Spread as flat as possible, using a wet spatula. Refrigerate for at least 2 hours.

Tip out onto a chopping board and portion into 15 rectangles. Store in the fridge until ready to use.

To cook, coat in plain flour, brushing off any excess then cook fry off in oil at 200°C for 5 minutes until crispy.

Tempura Batter

80g plain flour

80g cornflour

pinch table salt

200ml soda water

Whisk the flours and salt together. Add the soda water and whisk until smooth.

Tofu

500g soya milk

1 tablespoon olive oil

¾ teaspoon table salt

½ teaspoon caster sugar

1 teaspoon xanthan gum

1 teaspoon agar agar flakes

Place all ingredients into a medium sized saucepan. Bring to the boil, whisking continuously, for 3 minutes then reduce the heat to a simmer for 5 minutes. Place in a blender and blitz for 3 minutes. Pour into a plastic container and refrigerate for a minimum of 2 hours until set.

Miso tofu

Make as above but omit the salt and add 1 tablespoon white miso paste.

Sesame tofu

Make as per Tofu but substitute the olive oil for toasted sesame oil.

Zhoug

1 small bunch of coriander, leaves picked

½ small bunch of flat-leaf parsley, leaves picked

1 green chilli, deseeded and finely diced

½ teaspoon cumin seeds, toasted and finely crushed

1 cardamom pod, finely crushed

2 cloves, finely crushed

½ teaspoon agave syrup

2 garlic cloves, peeled and finely grated

50ml olive oil

½ teaspoon table salt

Put all the ingredients into a blender jug, with 2 tablespoons of water. Blend until a chunky paste is formed.

Sweet Tamarind Sauce

150g 100% tamarind paste

2 tablespoons soft dark brown sugar

1 tablespoon treacle

1 onion, peeled and finely diced

1 garlic clove, peeled and finely diced

½ teaspoon cumin seeds, toasted

½ teaspoon coriander seeds, toasted

½ teaspoon fennel seeds, toasted

1 cinnamon stick

2 star anise

4cm knob of ginger, peeled and finely grated

1 lemongrass stalk, finely grated microplaned

1 tablespoon tomato paste

1 tablespoon soy sauce

2 tablespoons white wine vinegar

Put all ingredients into a medium saucepan. Add 600ml water and bring the pan to a gentle simmer. Simmer slowly for 1 hour. Remove the cinnamon stick and star anise then blend the entire contents of the pan until smooth.

Spelt pasta

500g spelt flour
½ teaspoon table salt
225ml water
25g olive oil

Mix the spelt flour and salt together. Pour onto your bench and create a well in the centre. Mix the water and oil together then pour gently into the well. Knead the water into the flour until everything comes together and a smooth dough is formed. Form a ball with the dough, wrap in clingfilm and refrigerate for at least 30 minutes.

Plain Pasta

250g semolina flour
250g plain white flour
½ teaspoon table salt
225ml water
25g olive oil

Prepare the same way as above.

Black Sesame Pasta

50g black sesame seeds
25g sesame oil
225ml water
250g semolina flour
250g plain white flour
½ teaspoon table salt

Place the sesame seeds, sesame oil and half of the water into a blender and blend until a smooth paste is formed. Add the remaining water to the paste. Make the pasta as per the method in the spelt pasta recipe above, substituting the water and oil for the sesame mix.

Puff Pastry

200g strong flour
200g plain flour
½ teaspoon table salt
400g non-dairy butter
1 teaspoon lemon juice

Sift the flours and salt into a large bowl. Rub in 100g of the butter using your fingertips, until the mixture resembles breadcrumbs. Mix the lemon juice with 140ml iced water then add to the bowl and mix to form a stiff dough. Form into a ball, wrap in clingfilm and refrigerate for 30 minutes.

Roll out the pastry on a lightly floured worktop to form a rectangle about 30 x 20cm. Spread the remaining butter over the left half hand side of the pastry, leaving a border of 2cm around the edges. Fold the right half hand side of the pastry over the left half hand side to seal in the butter.

Now fold the last quarter of the pastry into the middle, and repeat with with the last quarter on the other side, so you have what looks like an open book. Then fold the 'book' in half lengthways. Place on a floured tray, cover with clingfilm, and refrigerate for 30 minutes.

Repeat the above step twice before rolling out and using as required.

Short Crust Pastry

200g plain flour
100g non-dairy butter
½ teaspoon table salt

Put the flour, butter and salt in a food processor and blitz until the mixture resembles breadcrumbs. Add just enough iced water to bind and process until just combined. Form into a ball, wrap in clingfilm and refrigerate for at least 30 minutes before using as required.

Rough Puff Pastry

250g non-dairy butter
250g plain white flour
½ teaspoon table salt

Sift the flour and salt into a bowl and partially rub in the butter, leaving small lumps. Bind together with 100–125ml of iced water – enough to form a stiff dough. Tip the dough onto a floured worktop and shape into a rectangle 4cm thick high. Transfer to a floured tray, cover with clingfilm, and refrigerate for 30 minutes.

Return the pastry to the floured worktop and roll into a rectangle measuring 20 x 15cm. Fold the last quarter of the pastry into the middle, and repeat with with the last quarter on the other side, so you have what looks like an open book. Then fold the 'book' in half lengthways. Transfer it back to the floured tray, cover with clingfilm, and refrigerate for 30 minutes. Repeat this step twice.

Finally, put the pastry rectangle on a floured worktop and roll out to 5mm thickness. Place on a baking tray lined with parchment paper and refrigerate for 30 minutes before using as required.

Soya Ricotta

130g dried soya beans, soaked overnight in 1 litre cold water
2 tablespoon olive oil
½ teaspoon table salt
1 teaspoon cider vinegar

If you have a soya milk maker, make the milk according to the manufacturer's instructions. Otherwise, rinse the soaked beans in fresh water then tip into a saucepan with 1 litre of warm water. Bring to a gentle simmer for 5 minutes. Blend the entire contents for 2 minutes then return to the saucepan and gently simmer for 20 minutes. Blend again, for 2 minutes. Return to the pan and simmer gently for a further 15 minutes. Blend continuously for 5 minutes.

Strain the milk through a nut milk bag, or a sieve lined with cheesecloth, into a bowl until all liquid has drained through been removed. Discard the remnants.

Put the soya milk in a medium saucepan over a moderate heat. Add the olive oil and salt and bring the milk to the boil. When boiling, add the vinegar then turn down the heat to a gently simmer. The milk will start to split, forming curds at the top. After 5 minutes, carefully pour the contents through a sieve lined with cheesecloth set over a bowl. Leave for 20 minutes then scrape out the cheese from the cheesecloth and refrigerate. You can use the whey too, so keep this in the fridge too.

Cashew Butter

200g cashew nuts
sea salt

Preheat the oven to 180°C/fan 160°C/gas mark 4. Spread the nuts on a baking sheet and bake for 10–12 minutes until deep golden. Tip into a container and cover with cold water and a good pinch of salt. Refrigerate overnight.

Strain and reserve the liquid. Put the soaked nuts in a blender with a quarter of the soaking water and blend until smooth. It should be a mousse-like peanut butter consistency – add more soaking liquid if necessary.

Almond butter

200g flaked almonds, toasted
¼ teaspoon table salt
50ml olive oil

Put the almonds, salt and half of the oil in a blender. Blend, adding the oil gradually, until it's a smooth paste.

Hazelnut butter

200g unskinned hazelnuts, toasted
¼ teaspoon table salt
50ml hazelnut or olive oil

Follow the instructions for the Almond Butter above.

Peanut butter

200g blanched peanuts, toasted
¼ teaspoon table salt

Blend the peanuts and salt with 50ml warm water. Keep adding water until you have a thick paste.

Onion Jam

50g non-dairy butter
4 onions, peeled and finely sliced
1 teaspoon table salt
25ml balsamic vinegar

Heat the butter in a large frying pan over a moderately high heat. When melted, add the onions and salt. Cook the onions until a deep golden colour, stirring regularly. Add the balsamic vinegar and cook for a further 5 minutes until all the liquid has evaporated and the onions are sticky.

Lemon curd

3 lemons
120g caster sugar
60g aquafaba
2 tablespoons cornflour
50g coconut oil
150g non-dairy butter

Zest one lemon and juice all three, into a medium sized saucepan. Add the sugar, aquafaba and cornflour and whisk well. Place over a moderate heat and cook, stirring continuously, for 20 minutes until the mix is thick and fluffy. Gradually, bit by bit, whisk in the coconut oil, and then butter, whisking well after each addition. Pass through a fine sieve into a clean container. Refrigerate.

Roast Garlic Aïoli

60g aquafaba
½ teaspoon Dijon mustard
2 tablespoons Roast Garlic Purée (see page 185)
175ml olive oil
1 tablespoon white wine vinegar
½ teaspoon table salt

Whisk the aquafaba, mustard and garlic together until combined. Slowly drizzle in the oil, little by little, whisking continuously until fully mixed. Season to taste.

Roast Garlic Purée

6 whole garlic bulbs
100ml olive oil
sea salt

Preheat the oven to 180°C/fan 160°C/gas mark 4.

Slice the tops off the garlic bulbs so that the cloves are just exposed. Place on a sheet of foil, on a baking sheet or roasting tray. Drizzle with 2 tablespoons of oil and sprinkle with salt. Gather the foil over the garlic to make a loose parcel then put the tray in the oven for 30 minutes then open the foil and cook for a further 15 minutes.

Remove from the oven and allow the bulbs to cool so you can handle them comfortably. Remove the outer layer of the bulb then squeeze out the roasted garlic from each clove into a blender jug. Add the remaining oil, with 2 tablespoons of warm water, and blend until smooth. Season to taste then refrigerate for up to 1 month.

Tahini verde

For the base
100g toasted sesame seeds
3 tablespoons sesame oil
½ teaspoon agave
75ml olive oil
50g chickpeas
juice of 1 lemon

2 tablespoons chopped tarragon leaves
2 tablespoons chopped coriander leaves
2 tablespoons chopped mint leaves
2 tablespoons chopped basil leaves
½ teaspoon table salt

Put the base ingredients in the jug of a blender and add 100ml cold water. Blend until smooth. Add the herbs and blend until a chunky paste is formed. Transfer to a jar and refrigerate.

Mustard Pickle

200ml white wine vinegar
80g caster sugar
2 tablespoons yellow mustard seeds
2 cloves
1 bay leaf

Put everything in a medium saucepan with 200ml water. Set the pan over a high heat and bring to the boil for 2 minutes. Remove from the heat and allow to cool.

Mayonnaise

30ml aquafaba
¼ teaspoon Dijon mustard
½ teaspoon white wine vinegar
230ml olive oil
⅛ teaspoon xanthan gum
table salt

Put the aquafaba in a medium mixing bowl. Add the mustard and vinegar and whisk until fluffy. Gradually drizzle in the olive oil, little by little, whisking continuously. Sprinkle the xanthan gum over the top of the olive oil and whisk vigorously until the mayonnaise thickens. Season to taste.

Basic Vinaigrette

3 tablespoons white wine vinegar
100ml olive oil
¼ teaspoon agave syrup
2 sprigs of tarragon

Put all the ingredients in a bowl and whisk together, allowing the tarragon to infuse the vinaigrette. Remove the sprigs before using. Always whisk or shake before use to ensure the mix has emulsified properly.

Sesame vinaigrette

3 tablespoons white wine vinegar
3 tablespoons toasted sesame oil
70ml olive oil
¼ teaspoon agave
1 teaspoon soy sauce

Put all the ingredients in a bowl and whisk together. Always whisk or shake before use to ensure the mix has emulsified properly.

Walnut vinaigrette

3 tablespoons white wine vinegar
2 tablespoons walnut oil
80ml olive oil
3 sprigs of thyme

Put all the ingredients in a bowl and whisk together, allowing the thyme to infuse the vinaigrette. Remove before using. Always whisk or shake before use to ensure the mix has emulsified properly.

Lemon vinaigrette

zest and juice of 1 lemon
100ml olive oil
1 teaspoon white wine vinegar
½ teaspoon agave syrup

Put all the ingredients in a bowl and whisk together. Always whisk or shake before use to ensure the mix has emulsified properly.

index

acknowledgements

Reflection upon gratitude is always a rather lovely thing to do, but depending on the time and place there are always different people at the forefront. Here are the thanks I feel are due at this point in time, but there are many, many more.

First and foremost thanks are to my family. I had the most wonderful, educational and experiential childhood which is such an important foundation. I am eternally grateful and humbled by it all.

To my first head chef, who took the time and effort to set me on this path, Craig Redmile, in NZ. To Josh Emmet, a million thanks for your support, guidance and constant belief in me, I don't think I would have stuck with it without your quiet encouragement at the beginning. And to Marcus, for giving me the opportunity to be me, and allowing me to grow and develop as a chef, an entrepreneur and a person. I have the utmost gratitude and admiration for your determination, focus, constant energy and drive to keep pushing the boundaries.

To the wonderful people who have become the Marcus Wareing Restaurants family. I would not be able to do what I do without all of you. I continue to be happily astounded by how you grow and develop and move forward. And a special thanks to team Tredwells, you all rock, and make me proud and grateful on a daily basis.

To Kyle. Thank you for allowing PLANTED to take flight. Your championing of it is incredible and I hope it does you proud. Here's to a well deserved time of smelling the daisies for you.

Thanks to Jonny & Hannah for being part of team CN! Thanks to Nassima for the gorgeous photos, and general lovely sparkle you bring to any room, along with Maria. Thanks for Becks for being so kick ass in the cooking department. Thanks to Wei and Lucy, for adding your creative genius and loveliness. Thanks to Beth, and Sam, for the support too.

Onwards, and upwards!